THE SKY IS a FREE COUNTRY

The Luminaire Award Anthology
Volume I

THE SKY IS a FREE COUNTRY

The *Luminaire* Award Anthology
Volume I

Winners & Placed Finalists
Poetry & Prose
Various Authors
Volume I Triennial:
2014-2016

Alternating Current Press
Boulder, Colorado

The Sky Is a Free Country
The Luminaire Award Anthology Triennial
Volume I: 2014-2016
Various Authors
©2016, 2019 Alternating Current Press

All material in *The Sky Is a Free Country* is the property of its respective creators and may not be used or reprinted in any manner without express permission from the authors or publisher, except for the quotation of short passages used inside of an article, criticism, or review. Printed in the United States of America. All rights reserved. All material in *The Sky Is a Free Country* is printed with permission.

Alternating Current
Boulder, Colorado
alternatingcurrentarts.com

ISBN-10: 1-946580-06-6
ISBN-13: 978-1-946580-06-1
First Edition: 2016
First Print Edition: February 2019

Table of Contents

Fiction

A Slow Dance in the Afternoon | Mia Eaker | 7
The Spirit of Shackleton | Gavin Broom | 14
For the Man after Me | Eric Shonkwiler | 22
The Poor Man's Guide to an Affordable, Painless Suicide | Schuler Benson | 32
Kinda Sorta American Dream | Steve Karas | 44
Sunrise Special | John Vicary | 54
The Elephant in the Bathtub | J. Lewis Fleming | 60
An American Seeker | Kevin Catalano | 72
Inheritance | Stephanie Liden | 80
Stoop | Alexa Mergen | 91
Sculpting Sand | Steve Karas | 98
Tennessee | Constance Sayers | 105
A Hindershot of Calion | Schuler Benson | 116

Poetry

Low Tide | Pete M. Wyer | 13
Miss Valley City, North Dakota | Charles P. Ries | 28
vii. (the leviathan) | Mary Buchinger | 30
William Barret Question Mark | CEE | 42
the thing is, you see | Normal | 43
Reign | Jared A. Carnie | 53
we move as dust | Mike Bernicchi | 58
After Abandon | Michael Cooper | 71
Sewing | Noel King | 78
Cause Célèbre | Andrei Guruianu | 79
Coralee Robbins Mafficks the Fall of Art | Amy Wright | 89
Birch Street | Charles P. Ries | 90
mob of one | Normal | 96
Baldwin Apples | Sarah Ann Winn | 104
With Apologies to Rose Bonne [The Halls of Ives] | CEE | 115

> *"The sky is filled with stars,
> invisible by day."*
> —Henry Wadsworth Longfellow

A Slow Dance in the Afternoon

Mia Eaker

Charles Hostettler arrived home early. His truck shrieked to a halt in the driveway of a small brick house nestled in the cul-de-sac on Laurel Avenue. His wife, Helene, wasn't expecting him home from work for another three hours. She heard his boots first, pounding up the front steps. Then, he barreled through the front door, slamming it behind him. He paused in the doorway. His eyes, wild and hazy, darted around the room.

The four women assembled in his living room, dressed primly in their Sunday best, sat frozen, eyes glued to the looming figure in the doorway. A young blonde, dressed in a pale pink sweater and beige slacks, was still leaning in, one elbow propped on her knee, gesturing with a pointed finger toward the woman sitting across from her. The other woman, who appeared much older, wore a honey-colored blouse with large pearl buttons. She sat straight, with deliberate posture; one knee was crossed carefully over the other. Her hands still held a slightly tilted pitcher and a half-full glass of iced tea.

In fact, the only pair of eyes not fixed on Charles belonged to Helene Hostettler. Her eyes, instead, stared straight down, right through the bottom of the empty glass in her hand and into the carpet below, as if the mingled heat and force from her gaze were strong enough to burn an escape route through the floor. Beside Helene sat a young woman who could not have been more than 25. Helene had determined this when she met her, although never asked. Helene had wondered whether the woman appeared so young to her because of her age or because of the way she dressed. Today, Meredith, the wife of the new pastor at their church, wore her hair pulled back in a ponytail with long curls that bounced when she walked. The dress was bright yellow from top to bottom, except for the white buttons. The color reminded Helene of warm sunshine on her face in the summer. The sleeves were cut off at the shoulders, exposing Meredith's long, slender arms.

Charles grunted in their direction and continued his rampage across the room and into the kitchen. Only a thin wall separated the four startled ladies from the heavy pounding of his boots back and forth on the tile floor. In the living room, the women sat in silence while the tension thickened in the air around them. The TV still played softly in the background. They'd been watching a ballroom-dance competition. Well, not really watching. Helene had turned it on and let it play quietly during the meeting because she liked to have background noise in the room. She was thankful for that noise now.

Above the quickening tempo of the music, the women tuned in to the excited clamor of cabinet doors opening and slamming shut, then jars and glasses clinking together. There was a brief silence. A hard thump against the refrigerator door. One by one, each lady shifted her concentration to missing items from purses, minutely crooked skirt seams that needed immediate attention, and imaginary last sips of coffee and tea from dry cup beds. On the other side of the wall, Charles finally collapsed into a chair, and a swift, sharp silence invaded the room and jolted the fidgety group to a halt.

Helene relaxed the clenched lines in her brow. Her hands remained calmly folded in her lap, the corners of her mouth tilted upward in a calculated and confident smile. After glancing toward the kitchen, she rolled her eyes and released a lighthearted chuckle. "Men," she sighed. "And they say women are emotional." Helene waved her hand through the air with a gesture intended to erase her husband's shocking tirade through the house just moments before.

Inside, even her bones were shaking. Her last sip of tea turned on her stomach. Cool beads of sweat seeped through her freshly ironed blouse. The ladies sitting around her smiled back, cautiously, wearing strained looks of understanding.

Finally, Meredith leaned over and patted Helene's hands gently. "Of course, sweetie. We all have one at home," she whispered, and added a wink for good measure.

Helene never met her eyes. Instead, she stared expressionless at Meredith's hopeful yellow dress. The dress annoyed her now because Meredith had worn it despite the growing cold outside and the winter season rolling in. Although Meredith had worn a heavy coat, Helene decided the dress was out of season and returned her attention to the other women.

"Maybe it's best to take a rain check on the rest of the meeting. I should really check on him," Helene noted and rose to her feet. "We've covered a lot. We could certainly talk after the service on Sunday about the last of the fundraiser plans," she added reassuringly.

The three other women promptly fussed with purses, cell phones, and jackets. As they herded toward the door, Charles emerged from the kitchen. His movements had been silent and calm. He appeared without warning, without so much as the scuff of his feet on floor. He wore a smile now, a smile that was new and warm.

"My apologies, ladies, for the outburst," he said. "I had forgotten that Helene was having company today. Work was quite a mess," he chuckled. "Too much excitement, but it's no excuse. Helene and I are happy to have you." He spoke with a chilling calm, his words lyrical and soothing. Charles looked head-on at each of the bewildered faces in front of him. "It's too bad that we have plans for dinner with my boss, or I'd ask if you'd like to stay for supper," he noted matter-of-factly, yet pleasantly and with an air of regret.

When his transformed gaze met Helene's, he extended his arm toward her, and she folded into his embrace without so much as a pause. Their eyes locked for a moment before Helene turned to face the other women. "Ah, how silly of me. I completely forgot about that. I guess it's just as well," she said, and gestured to the front door.

The women glided to it and filed into an obedient line. Helene smiled and hugged each of her friends, thanking them for coming. In turn, each of her friends left with a sincere "thank you" for the refreshments and an assurance that, like her forgotten dinner plans, there was a necessary engagement or to-do list waiting to be taken care of as soon as they left.

Meredith gave Helene's hand a gentle squeeze and peered over her shoulder toward the kitchen. She started to speak, but hesitated. Instead, she looked down at Helene's hand lying in hers and scuffed her foot on the brick step where she stood. Meredith looked back toward the kitchen, where Charles had retired, with a determined gaze and stammered loudly, "I'll see you *both* at church on Sund—"

"You'd better get going," Helene cut in. "A pastor's wife has lots to do." She smiled at Meredith reassuringly and released her hand.

Meredith responded with an uncertain grin, her cheeks quivering slightly. Then, she nodded, turned, and went to her car, the hem of her sunshine-colored dress still peering out from under her winter coat. Helene twisted her mouth into a subtle scowl as she watched Meredith shut the car door and slip her keys into the ignition. Helene's feet remained glued to the front steps while Meredith's car eased down the road and disappeared onto the highway. Helene stood in the doorway, breathing in the calm, crisp air outside and letting it linger around her a little longer. Then, she closed the front door and walked over to the window and quietly pulled the blinds. She turned to face the kitchen and found Charles already in the doorway.

"Why were they here, Helene?" He was leaning against the doorframe, hands shoved in his pockets.

She didn't jump when he appeared there suddenly. She had learned to turn every corner with the expectation that he'd be standing there. He often appeared from other rooms, from around nearby corners, or even from behind her.

"Church meeting. We have a fundraiser to plan," Helene replied, quick and confident with her words. "We decided on a bake sale and raffle," she added with a cheerful grin that nearly cramped her cheeks. "Did you know the rain flooded the park? That's where we planned to have the meeting. Meredith called this morning and asked if they could swing by here, instead."

Although Helene was careful to hold his gaze, she now noted that his hands were no longer in his pockets. One fist was clenched. She knew better than to look directly at anything except his eyes when he was angry.

She had been in love with Charles when she married him five years before, when everything was peaceful. The yelling hadn't started until nearly a year ago, just after his father, to whom he hadn't spoken in years, died suddenly in a car accident. Charles hadn't hit her until a few months ago. The bruise on her arm was easy enough to cover up. She'd had to become more creative since then—makeup tricks, jackets, accessories, illness, whatever she could think of that she was pretty sure she hadn't used more than once before. Over the last few months, she'd also developed an ability of nearly superhero proportion to take in every movement of his body, every expression change, even the scope of the room, without averting her eyes or losing the casual, singsong flow of her voice.

"It was after you left for work, and I didn't want to bother you," she explained, feeling a quiver in her throat. "I didn't think you'd be—"

"—home so early," he cut in sharply, sliding a foot in her direction.

Helene took a step away from him, gliding her feet toward the coffee table and lifting the silver tray gingerly from the end table. She cleared away the glasses and coffee cups, stacking them on the tray with careful attention. "I see that, sweetie. What happened at work?" In truth, she already knew. Layoffs had been happening at the factory for weeks, causing Charles to be increasingly stressed, and increasingly angry.

From the doorway, Charles only continued to stare, clenching his fist tighter.

"It came today, didn't it? The notice?" She let the words drag slowly and sweetly from her lips, tilting her face slightly so he could see it and pinching her eyebrows together to mark her concern. She stood carefully and tiptoed backward, holding a tray of empty coffee cups and glasses. With her right hand, she slipped a large glass off of the tray and behind her back. The glass, embellished with yellow flower petals, had a subtle crack etched in its side.

"Why do you think it came?" Charles stuttered. His eyes darkened. "You assume that I got fired. I'm not a lazy-ass like some of the other guys there. I work hard, and I've been there for more years than most. I *deserve* to be there!" He paused, still glaring at her. "But, of course, you don't think so." His voice shook. His eyes, already red and swollen, widened in fury. "It's just like you to assume the worst of me!" His words struggled to find air through a barrage of powerful, desperate sobs. He reached for the lamp on the table next to him and ripped its cord from the wall. Then, in one massive, thunderous swoop, he buried the bottom edge in the living room wall.

Helene screamed, dropping the tray to the floor and ducking behind the recliner on the far end of the room. Shards of bright yellow flower-printed glass decorated the floor all around her. She sat, crouching behind the chair, listening to Charles grunt and curse as he wrestled the lamp out of the wall.

Waiting.

Charles kicked the wall with the steel toe of his boot and then pounded it with his fists.

Somewhere in the background, subtle and indistinct, Helene heard the rising echo of clapping and cheering. The dancers on TV leaped back into her mind. The music. The clapping. She couldn't see the screen from her hiding place, only the walls blocking her in from every side. She strained to focus her ears on anything other than the sound of Charles, ten feet away, now tugging violently at the lamp lodged in the wall and shouting obscenities that sent shivers rushing down her spine.

On the TV, a new couple sauntered onto the floor to the sound of cheering. The applause stopped. The couple was ready. As the music started up softly, Helene rocked back and forth. She wrapped her arms around her knees and closed her eyes. Huddled over, Helene was more than afraid. She was ashamed. Ashamed that she'd taken a chance. Ashamed that she believed him a week ago when he said things were going to be different. With her eyes closed tight, she saw herself floating right through the wall and stepping into the grass where she'd be out of his reach. Slipping into woods where he couldn't find her. She pictured wings blooming from her shoulders and carrying her up into clouds where she'd be free. She felt herself slowly dissolving into the air until she could imagine being invisible to him.

Her breath came a little easier, deeper and less shaky. It slowed in tune to music that now seemed to fill the room. A calm acceptance flooded over and through her, and her shaking bones stilled. She opened her eyes and reached for the remaining bottom half of the glass she had been holding behind her back. Her finger traced the lines along the yellow flower petals and the sparkling jagged spikes that wrapped around the top like a holiday wreath.

The lamp suddenly exploded from the wall. Her fingers clutched the base of the glass. Her eyes stared straight into the pile of broken shards in front of her. Charles moved in her direction. Helene listened to his every movement. The slow, controlled shuffle of his boots as they neared. The smell of his cologne and sweat. The chuckling in his belly. The rhythmic tap of his finger against the metal base of the lamp. The familiar pulse of his anger when it began to rise. The quickening thump in her chest. The music. Helene drifted away, dissolved into the air.

The broken glass crunched on the other side of the chair, and Helene thought she glimpsed the toe of a boot. She shivered, clutching the base of the cracked glass even tighter in her palm. She squeezed it between her fingers until her anger matched his, until she leaped to her feet and stood with her eyes staring straight into his. Her rage clashed with his, and it merged in the air between them. She felt it. Heard it. It crackled like twisted flames bursting from a campfire. His arm shot into the air; the base of the lamp flashed as it peaked above her head.

Helene swung. The broken glass struck Charles at the base of his neck. His eyes widened and locked with hers, and Helene released a desperate cry into the room. Charles shrieked in pain and surprise as he crumpled to the floor. Helene followed him, dropping to her knees beside him and pressing her hands over the wound in his neck.

"I'm sorry," she whispered. "I'm so sorry." She moved one hand from the wound to reach for the phone on the end table. "I'm calling an ambulance. You're gonna be fine," she sobbed, barely able to get the words out. Tears gathered on her husband's cheeks. With one hand he held her arm, and with the other, gripped the hem of her skirt. Helene and Charles locked their eyes as if they were in an embrace, an embrace that held fast while Helene called for the ambulance, while she removed her blouse and pressed it against his wound, while they waited. Neither of them looked away.

Low Tide

Pete M. Wyer

We were used to the rhythm of tides.
We'd sat by calm water,
Been ruffled by restless winds.
We didn't suspect
The rotted wrecks
Caught among the jagging rocks
That steered the course of the river,
Starkly revealed by this day.

He closes his eyes.
We, his friends,
Sit in silence.

The Spirit of Shackleton

Gavin Broom

When the police told me to start from the beginning, I explained that it had started on a Tuesday night in July, on the evening of the full moon. Of course, it must've really started much earlier than that—weeks, maybe months, earlier—but that Tuesday night was the one that stuck in my brain. The cops nodded their approval and invited me to continue, which I did, just as soon as I'd crushed out my thirtieth cigarette of the day.

A medley of painkillers had done nothing to shift my headache, so I stood on the back patio, nursing a joint and a Scotch and hoping that would do the trick instead. The huge moon hung just above the hills like a balloon waiting to be popped, and I found that, while I stared at it, and while I listened to the chirruping of the grasshopper orchestra playing on the prairie, my headache may not have been getting better, but at least it had stopped getting worse.

"You okay, Dad?" a little voice asked.

"Me? Yeah, I'm cool, Zander," I said, forcing a smile. As casually as possible, I let the joint drop to the ground and covered it with a tan sandal. "I'm cool. What makes you ask?"

"I thought I heard you and Mom fighting."

It surprised me to find that I couldn't remember much of the specifics of the argument, even though its echoes were still fresh. I suspected the official cause was something to do with the faulty TiVo or the fact that the maid hadn't shown up for the last couple of days or that the maid had been the one who'd fucked up the TiVo in the first place. I couldn't remember. What I did remember was plummeting into a foul mood after I'd come off a conference call with the Mumbai office an hour earlier, and this probably magnified whatever Melissa had done to piss me off. I would have asked for her opinion, but she was so drunk that any real inquiry or apology would need to wait until morning, and by that time, it would no longer matter.

I sipped my drink and changed the subject. "Isn't it funny how we always see the same side of the moon?"

"Huh?" Zander asked.

"You know. The moon. It's always the same side that shines down on us. It's more obvious when it's as big as it is tonight. It's just weird, don't you think?" The dope, it seemed, was starting to take effect.

"It used to spin, Bryan," he said with a sigh, bored and calling me by my first name. "Like, years ago. But it's in synchronous rotation now that Earth's gravity has slowed it down and stuff. And the moon's no bigger tonight than it was last night; it's just because it's so near the horizon that you have a focal reference, instead of it being high in the sky surrounded by stars."

A minute passed while I kept my eyes dead ahead at what I now understood to be a regular-sized moon.

"Nothing escapes gravity, Dad. Not even the moon."

"What age are you, Zander?"

"Nine."

"Nine years old," I said with a whistle. "How'd you get so clever?" I looked down at my son and ruffled his hair.

Ignoring this attention, the boy shrugged and took a hit from his asthma inhaler, even though he hadn't been wheezing. "I read up on it. It's part of my special project."

I took a moment to replay anything I may have already heard about this project to decide if asking about it now would be an admission of ignorance. By the time I'd decided to keep my mouth shut on the matter and let Zander explain if he wanted, he had already given up and gone indoors.

The brief conversation went out of my head, until the next morning at breakfast. Zander had just taken his baryta carbonica pill—something Melissa had recently prescribed to help with his bashfulness—and was about to leave for school, when Rayne, our neighbor's eight-year-old kid, came into the kitchen. I've never liked Rayne, mostly because he's a boy with a girl's name. With the maid being MIA, I wondered who'd let the little sissy in.

"Good morning, Mrs. Carlyle," Rayne said to Melissa. He spun toward me like a mini maître d'. "Mr. Carlyle."

I nodded and scowled.

"Good morning, Rayne," Melissa drawled, making me think she was already drunk. "Are your parents still having their barbecue tonight?"

Rayne looked confused. "I think it's Ocean's parents who're having the party, Mrs. Carlyle." He gave himself a quick blast from his own inhaler, which was a different color than Zander's. I didn't know if this meant his asthma was more or less serious, so I made a note to look into it later.

Melissa's head nodded in a wide circle, and she waved her spoon at our guest. "Yes, of course. Tell them we're looking forward to it."

Appearing even more confused, Rayne walked over to Zander, who was loading up his bag with binders, books, his Omega-3-rich lunchbox, and his little plastic tray of medical supplies. The two of them whispered to each other, chattering excitedly, drifting in and out of earshot.

"I'm Captain," Zander insisted, and his buddy nodded in agreement. "You guys are crew."

"You talking about your bassoon recital?" I tried, hoping I'd guessed the correct instrument.

Rayne started to giggle. I really hated that kid.

"Project stuff, Dad," Zander said, throwing his bag over his shoulder. "Don't sweat it. Can I have fifty bucks?"

As soon as I heard the door close—and with my wallet fifty dollars lighter—I asked Melissa if she had any idea what this special project was all about.

She stared through me for ages, still waving her spoon as she contemplated an answer. "I think it's got something to do with ..."

When it became clear that she had no intention of finishing her sentence, I retreated to my office where I spent an hour looking at Internet pornography, and then, I phoned Mumbai and took my temper out on them.

Ocean's parents are the biggest hippies on Buena Vista Drive, and because the whole family is vegetarian, Darryl cooked peppers and potatoes on the barbecue and served it with tofu, falafel, and hummus on the side. I'd have killed the cow myself, if it meant I would have gotten a burger.

The conversation was pretty standard, and, within an hour—with the coyotes over the hill baying either their approval at the rising moon or their disappointment at the absence of meat—we'd squeezed the life from all the usual topics. Melissa had rhymed off the benefits of the new homeopathic meds she'd discovered on the Internet. Rachel, a romance writer and Rayne's mom, had played some MP3s of Rayne's bassoon-playing over the external B&O sound system. After a lot of cajoling from Darryl, Ocean had demonstrated her flexibility with a highly accomplished yoga routine, and then, not even in a sweat, she'd gone off with the other kids to play Wii or whatever. That apart, we covered the same old PTA issues, our offspring's asthma, taxes, work, smog levels in the city, and all the usual shit. I excused myself three times to take imaginary conference calls from Mumbai.

After a while, the two other men and I escaped to the far end of the garden, beyond the pool, and we all helped Darryl get through his stash of weed and whiskey. The women stayed at the table near the barbecue, and while we waited in silence for Darryl to skin up, I could hear Melissa repeat her meds stories. I stared at the moon and tried to ignore her.

"Hey, Bryan," Rayne's old man, a fifty-something accountant named Garfield, said. "It's good to see our boys get on so well."

"Sure is, Gar," I agreed. Part of me hated to admit it, but it seemed Melissa's prescription of bar-c had very much helped Zander overcome his shyness and anxiety, and he'd made friends with all the neighborhood kids. I remembered the conversation from breakfast. "Do you know anything about a special project they're working on?"

Garfield shook his head. "Should I?"

I shrugged.

Darryl, toking deeply on his spliff, managed to wheeze, "I know."

We waited thirty seconds for him to exhale and continue.

"He's got Ocean involved in it, too," he explained. "I overheard her a couple of nights ago."

"Involved in what?" I asked, pissed that this doofus seemed to know more than I. "Overheard what? Is it school work?"

"Don't think so, dude. I think it's Zander's project."

If someone was ringleader, it was bound to be Zander. I'm Captain, he'd said that morning.

"So, what is it?" I asked, sounding calmer than I was feeling.

But by this time, Darryl had taken another toke and passed the J on to Garfield, and before he was in a position to continue, some commotion from the women's end of the garden disturbed us. Melissa and Rachel were leaning over the fence, looking into our yard, and they appeared to be in conversation with someone on the other side. A loud clank of metal finally perked my curiosity enough to abandon the guys and the dope and walk up the garden to find out what the hell was going on. When she saw me approach, Melissa came to meet me halfway.

"You've got some explaining to do, mister," she said. "Your son..."

"Our son what?"

"Your son tells me you gave him fifty bucks to buy scrap metal. What did you do that for? Do you have any idea the disease that's carried on metal?"

"You were there when I did it," I spat. "You handed me my wallet."

Sure enough, when I got to the fence and looked over, Rayne and Ocean were shuffling large strips of what looked like aluminum into our yard with help from Cambridge and Tuesday, the twin boy and girl from across the street. I could never remember which one was which. Zander, meanwhile, directed traffic up to the back fence.

"You said it was okay, Bryan," Zander shouted over to me.

A hand landed on my shoulder, and when I saw its owner, I was faced with Darryl's puffed cheeks and pinking eyes.

"I overheard Ocean talking on her cell phone," he said. "They're building a spaceship."

Over the next few days, the construction of the spaceship continued to take shape at the far end of our yard, and it wasn't long before my expectations were wrecked. Despite the arrival of large quantities of sheet metal, I still had an image of a box racer decorated with crayon-drawn flags on cardboard wings. Instead, the framework reminded me of a cigar tube that had been squashed and fattened out.

"That's a rocket, Dad," Zander told me without looking at me, after I'd explained my preconceptions. It was a Sunday, and he was in the yard, dressed in a suit, focused on some blueprints on a clipboard. "We're not building a rocket. We're building a spaceship."

"Is there a difference?"

He scratched his head with the cartridge end of his asthma inhaler. "There's no cardboard in my plans."

"Touché."

"Y'know, Dad? We could really use another fifty bucks."

And while I didn't ever see the kids doing anything other than hammering a few random panels, gradually more and more detail was added to the construction until it became clear that there were actually two parts to it, and the spaceship was poised on a platform that pointed toward the hills where the coyotes howled at night. Soon, even Melissa noticed.

"I'm worried about how this project is affecting Zander's bassoon playing," she said, once a door and porthole had appeared on the ship. "He and Rayne are supposed to be playing a recital for the community leaders' fundraiser, and he hasn't prepared. Neither of them has. Ocean's been learning the sitar for nothing."

"The community leaders can kiss my ass," I said, not really knowing what I meant by that, but feeling I had to express outrage at something.

My outburst shocked Melissa enough to make her retreat to the bedroom with a blender full of margarita.

Two days later, and as the finishing touches were being applied to the ship, a ten-foot by five-foot LED display unit perched itself on the far fence. A day after that, and the kids had it working.

73 hours, 00 minutes, 01 second.

73 hours, 00 minutes, 00 seconds.

72 hours, 59 minutes, 59 seconds.

Because it kept ticking down, it took me an embarrassingly long time to calculate when the red digits on the timer would reach zero, but after a while, I came up with my answer: nine o'clock on Friday evening. By that time, the numbers had totally freaked me out, but the only drugs I could find in the house were Zander's expired Ritalin from a couple years ago when we suspected he had ADHD. If anything, they made me feel worse.

I didn't really sleep that night, and the next day, when I phoned Mumbai, I was fucking unbearable and a bit racist.

When there were 28 hours left on the display, all the parents received an invitation to the launch, produced on homemade, organic paper and printed in such a way that it looked like handwriting. Rachel thought the whole thing was a hoot—that was what she called it—and even Melissa had started to chill out about the idea.

"Our children have such imagination," she said.

"From what I hear," Darryl said, "it's all your Zander's handiwork. He's the brains behind the operation."

"They're all taking it so seriously." Gar leaned forward, swaying in everyone's face. "Aren't they? When was the last time they took something so seriously? I wish we could get Rayne to apply himself in his Japanese cookery class as much as this. He's really let that slip recently."

I've tasted the little brat's California rolls and, to be honest, I've never thought they were any good—certainly not restaurant quality.

Rachel hugged herself and smiled. "It's good to see them all getting along so well. I mean, it can't be easy for them, you know?"

Everyone nodded. I suspected I wasn't alone in not having the first clue what she meant.

When Friday morning arrived, and I looked out into the yard, the only work being carried out on the spaceship was by one of the interchangeable twins who was polishing it up. Other than that, it looked finished. By the afternoon, the shine had been worked to such a level, it was like someone had laid a tubed mirror out on an angled sun lounger. Whenever I peeked out from my office, the reflection from the sun fried my eyes, and when I turned back indoors, everything was blue.

The kids—Zander, Rayne, Ocean, Tuesday, and Cambridge—hustled toward Zander's room with a couple of hours to go. They were all dressed smartly in Armani with black ties and Ray-Bans. Each of them, even Zander, had a silver case that each wheeled behind himself. I was sure they'd all had haircuts since the last time I'd seen them. Melissa clasped her heart as they marched through the house.

"Adorable," she said. "Aren't they just so grown up?"

The adults all arrived shortly after. I'd gotten a case of domestic beer—I dunno, it just seemed fitting—and we stood outside like a bunch of assholes and watched the countdown fall toward the inevitable, while the sun did the same.

Seemingly to mark every passing of five minutes, someone would say something like, "Isn't this exciting?" or "I can't wait," or "It's just like New Year's ... takes forever to get to midnight, then, it's suddenly, like, three a.m." I didn't add to the collection of bon mots and instead, made sure I got more than my share of the beer. When I collected up some empties, I noticed a hint of tequila from Melissa's cans.

0 hours, 6 minutes, 27 seconds.

In the moments leading up to the launch, the sun gave up the ghost and was replaced by a blushing moon that looked too big and heavy to creep any further up the sky. Then, I remembered Zander's words from last Tuesday and realized my eyes were just playing tricks on me. Once the countdown had tripped over five minutes, the French doors slid open, and the five figures emerged from the house to rapturous applause from the parents.

They were all dressed in foil suits, each with a badge sewn on the upper arm that had the words, *The Spirit of Shackleton*, written around a drawing of Earth, and they wore what looked like cartoon fishbowls on their heads. Beneath the bowls, their new haircuts were covered by white hoods, making them all look uniform and asexual. As they walked to the spaceship and waved back at us, I noticed for the first time in months how young and small and childlike they all looked, how they were all kids, not even in double digits, and it made me a little ashamed and teary and frightened because they were all so fragile.

I presumed it was Zander who led the way up the ramp and opened the door, but it could've been any of them. Whoever it was took one last look back to us, saluted, and then, disappeared inside. Within a minute, the others had all followed suit.

"Hey, Bryan," Garfield said, raising his beer can to me. "You didn't buy them gas, did you? I'm kinda expecting this sucker to take off!"

"You're thinking of a rocket," I whispered. "This is a spaceship."

No one heard me, though, as they were too busy roaring with laughter. Melissa, drunker than anyone else, thanks to her tequila-beer combo, watched the scene with one eye shut and a slurpy kind of liquid grin on her face. Gar high-fived with Darryl, and then they crashed their beer cans together, sending up a geyser of suds. Rachel bounced up and down on the tips of her toes and clapped her hands just in front of her nose and mouth. Cambridge's and Tuesday's folks, who had been making asses of themselves for the last hour, had brought novelty foam hands and were whooping like they were at a ballgame. I think I was the only one frozen to the spot, my mouth dried out and cold, my eyes glassing over.

0 hours, 0 minutes, 10 seconds.

"Ten!" everyone shouted.

0 hours, 0 minutes, 9 seconds.

"Nine!"

And so it continued, and I watched with an increasing sense of dread and a desire to run over to the timer and pull the plug, except from where I stood, I couldn't see a plug. I took some comfort from the fact that there was no steam or flames coming from the back of the ship.

0 hours, 0 minutes, 3 seconds.

"Three!"

0 hours, 0 minutes, 2 seconds.

"Two!"

0 hours, 0 minutes, 1 second.

"One!"

―⁓⁓―

Nothing happened.

The second it had taken to trip down from one had been the longest of my life, but now, I was looking at a line of flashing zeros and nothing had happened. Absolutely nothing.

0 hours, 0 minutes, 0 seconds.

I took one step toward Zander's spaceship.

Then, it disappeared.

I don't mean there was a plume of smoke or steam or dry ice. I don't mean a canvas dropped in front of them. One instant, they were there; the next, we were all staring at an empty platform with a blinking display behind it. They fucking vanished. They were gone.

"Where …"

I had no idea who had spoken. Maybe it was one of the adults. Maybe it was all of them. Maybe it was I. Whoever had said it pretty much summed up everything we were all feeling, and that one word was the cue for chaos.

The women pounced forward toward the ramp. Tuesday's and Cambridge's mom, still wearing her foam hand, ran onto the platform where the spaceship had been just seconds earlier, looking down as though she were expecting to see a miniaturized version of them scuttling around. Melissa fell to the ground, and for a moment, I thought she was searching underneath the platform for a trap door or something, and perhaps to begin with, that was exactly what she was doing. By the time I got to her, she was howling and pounding the concrete slabs beneath her, screaming unintelligible garbage into the ground. Gar grabbed me by my shirt and shook me.

"Where are they, Carlyle?" he roared. "What the fuck have you done with our kids?"

I waited for a punch that didn't arrive, and eventually, he let go of my shirt, threw his arms around me, and started crying on my shoulder. Some time later, someone—Ocean's mom, perhaps—called the cops and reported our kids missing, but by that time, I had figured it out. They weren't missing, and they weren't coming back, and they would never be found. Zander had worked out a way to beat gravity. He was the captain, and the others were his crew. They'd abandoned us. In the sky, the moon—while shining brighter than it had ever been before—suddenly looked very small and very far away.

―⁓⁓―

And so, when they asked me to take it from the top, just one more time, that was what I told the cops. I started at the beginning, and I finished at the end, and every single word I said in between was true.

FOR THE MAN AFTER ME

Eric Shonkwiler

The chains on the Ranger quiet and go silent altogether when he pulls up behind the wreck. There is a long, curling drag of snow ahead like the beginning of a figure-eight or from far above, maybe the top of a cursive letter, e or a, except it ends with the blue Explorer smashed driver-side into the telephone pole. Just take the rims, he thinks, if they aren't factory. A TapOut necklace is swinging gently from the rearview, and he stills it. He could just go on. He could call 911 and leave. If there's someone inside, don't mess with it. Leave it for the cops.

It's a new snow, and the clouds have already passed after dropping a couple inches, and the sky is bright blue. The cold cuts through his Carhartt to his back, and he can feel it spasming, and he wants to lie down, feels the lack of sleep in his shoulders from staying up with Brendan after his nightmare. The back windows on the Explorer are tinted, and he can't see inside. He steps off the road and into the packed snow, over the dirt and grass kicked up from the skid, and peers in the passenger window. The impact cracked the windshield, and the airbag is drooping toward an empty seat. He breathes. He looks down at his feet for footprints and sees some intricate sneaker tracks leading up to the road. He pulls his cell from his coat pocket and dials up the shop.

MD answers. New meat. What you got for me?

'96 Explorer. It's in bad shape.

Gonna need a rollback?

He walks around the other side of the truck. It's curved like a fish, and the driveshaft has to be crooked. Yeah, he says, and nods like MD will see.

You just find it?

Yeah. There's no one around. He puts his hand on the hood. Engine's still a bit warm.

Where you at?

He tells him.

We'll be out. Sit tight.

They hang up. There's no one coming either direction, and he can just barely hear the semis on 29. From this far off, they don't sound like trucks, and all he really hears is the hum of them passing, like whales, he imagines, the sound of displacement. He briefly remembers a book he'd read in elementary school, the word "cetacea" above pictures of whales, row on row, all shapes and sizes, before walking around to the front of the wreck. There's less wind from this side, and he puts his hands on his hips and arches his back, feels it strain, crack. He kneads the muscle beside the spine with his knuckles. He walks a few feet into the field to see if the telephone pole is cracked, but it's fine, not even crooked from what he can see. He wonders how the poles are strung a hundred feet apart, yet people always seem to hit them, never pass on through into the field or to someone's yard, something harmless. The glass is busted out from the driver-side window, and the bits look like blue-green gems sprinkled in the snow. The rest of the truck seems intact. At the back, gauging the trueness of the vehicle with one eye, like judging a pool cue, it doesn't seem as bad as he first thought.

He looks up and sighs, scans the horizon. Cornfields for a couple hundred acres, and then to the south, thick woods. If it were tomorrow, it would be deer season, and he'd hear nothing but gunshots. Maybe still the hums of 29. It's a good day for picking, he's told, if you're careful. Find a truck at the edge of a field and take the rims, take the battery if there's time. He jumps the short ditch and starts back to his Ranger but stops. There is a tiny flag of red floating against the trees. He squints, visors his hand over his eyes. It's red, not orange, so not some eager hunter. The footprints below him go from the passenger door to the road, stop where the snow is mostly gone in the center, and continue into the field. He yells for the person, a long hey, hands cupped. The red doesn't get any closer or further, only seems to sway a little.

He looks both ways down the road, still abandoned, and starts to highfoot it across the cornfield, the broken stover catching and tripping him up every few steps. Now, he can see it's a woman, wearing one of those sweater-vests. He can make out the white of her turtleneck and her jeans. He yells again, starting to breathe heavily, and waves. She's just standing there, walking a tight circle. She's not even looking up. He doesn't see any blood, and wonders how she could have gotten away without a scratch. Then she pivots for the rest of her circle, and, right before he can grab her by the shoulders, he sees her eyes. The left is blown, all the wiry capillaries burst, and her iris is thin blue but wildly bright against the blood.

Ma'am, he says, are you all right?

He's stopped her now and is holding tight to her shoulders. She doesn't say anything. He looks her up and down and still sees nothing wrong with her, just the eye. He remembers his phone and looks back at the vehicles a hundred yards away. He pulls his phone out and calls MD.

Cancel it, man, he says. The driver's out here, and I need to call her an ambulance.

The woman grabs his arm. I'm looking for my dog.

He stares at her. For a moment, she's in profile, and he notices she's pretty, delicate nose, long eyelashes, a classy everymom sort of haircut. Lady, your dog ain't here. He turns back to the phone. You got a pre-pay to call on or anything?

Yeah, MD says. Where were you again?

Lewis Road, probably a mile or two back from 29.

She know who you are?

I don't think she knows who she is, he says.

We could keep rollin'.

He stops, looks at the ground. You won't beat the medic out, will you?

No. She make it if we wait?

He glances back at her. I got no idea, man. Her eye's all fucked up, and she's talking about a dog. I think she's in shock or something.

Well. MD sighs. We could use a '96.

He curses softly, turns in his tracks. The woman has started her circle again. All right, I'll deal with it. She's moving around okay.

Your boy called a bit ago.

He smiles briefly. I just taught him the number.

He's smart, huh?

Yeah, he ain't nothin' like me. Look, I better go.

Sure, kid.

He pockets the phone. Come on, ma'am. Get you out of the cold.

He takes the woman's arm, and he has to pull to get her to move. She's still warm somehow. They don't get far before she tumbles in the rough dirt and snow, and they both go down. As he lifts up, he hears a car coming and lowers back to his chest, his hands covered in snow and his chin almost touching it. A Sunfire heading toward 29. It slows, stops. He should have put his hazards on. He should have taken off the back plate. He should have made the drive to the shop and asked for one of their cars. The Sunfire goes on after a few seconds.

Jesus. He feels the sweat on his forehead freeze. He gets up and brushes his hands on the front of his coat. The woman is facedown and unmoving. Lady. Hey. She doesn't respond. Hey. He grips her shoulder, rolls her over. Are you okay? You hurt? There's no answer again, so he throws her arm over his shoulder and stands with her, and once her feet are under her, she begins to move. He hears air like she's trying to whistle or maybe whisper, and he stops and says, What?

But she keeps on. Her lips are pursed oddly, and he realizes she is just breathing, and he feels something weighing him down inside. When they reach the road, he puts a little distance between them, and she drops onto the pavement and snow.

Shit.

He moves his arms in a wave, unsure, and looks down the road even as he angles toward her. She is crumpled up on herself like her legs became unboned. He turns her head to look at him, the red eye strong and piercing, and he almost has to cover it to keep looking at her. The skin of her face has gone pale, cool as the snow. He presses at her neck, tries to find a pulse. He checks her wrist in a panic. He can't tell. To the east, the road is still clear, and he brushes away at the snow stuck to her vest and creeping into the folds of her turtleneck. The Sunfire didn't get his plate; he's sure. Not hers, either. Just checking out a crash. He can leave now. He can call 911 and have them come get her and be gone, headed home. Take the O2 sensors and battery and the rims and be gone and have something to give MD. But there are his tracks, truck, and footprints, and if someone gets curious, he could get ID'd. He pulls her half up, thinking maybe she'll start moving again once she's standing, but feels her still slack and heavy on his shoulder, and he bends to sweep her legs up and staggers with her toward his Ranger. Something buzzes against his chest, and he figures it's her phone. Drive her in, then. Meet the ambulance. Keep it away from the scene so the guys can scoop up the wreck. Nothing to be done. He's a Samaritan, not a thief. Can even be anonymous.

He has to set her down to open the door, pressing his knees to the quarter panel and trapping her partly against it with his arm, keeping her from the ground, then lifting her up and nearly losing his balance putting her in the seat. His cheek presses against her breast, and he catches perfume and feels embarrassed more than anything before looking at her face, head lax, leaning toward him. He is only now really afraid and only now because she is dead, and he doesn't know what that means. He pushes her toward the center of the bench seat and closes the door quickly so it doesn't end up slamming her head if she slouches back.

With his hands free and walking around the front of the Ranger, he starts to shake. The Explorer is motionless—as though it should be moving. Caught like a still of a movie, and there should be glass flying through the air if he looked hard enough. The road is empty as far as he can see, and he opens his door and gets in, turns the key. The truck starts up and the radio blares metal, and he is embarrassed again. As he pulls the wheel hard to the left, he has the feeling that he's fleeing a crime scene.

He puts it up to fifty comfortably before thinking he hasn't buckled her in, and he hits the brakes. She lurches, head striking the dash. He winces and rights her, clips her seatbelt.

I'm sorry, he says, and brushes her hair back to straighten it, like someone will notice or care.

Going on toward 29, he looks over at her every couple hundred feet to see if maybe she's come back around, but she hasn't. He stops at the intersection, scans her, grabs her wrist to see if it's warm again. Her eyes are open and looking blankly at the floor or her lap. The left eye looks peeled. He wants to push her head back against the seat because it seems more comfortable that way. There's a buzz, and he remembers her phone. It vibrates musically, two short buzzes and a long one, then again, again. He lets it go and turns left.

The firehouse is in the center of town, just past the stoplight, he remembers. It's been a while since he's been here, the last time he came to an away football game. The phone buzzes again after they enter the village limits, and he leans over, eyes still on the road, and searches through her vest pocket for it. He pulls it out and looks at it. The picture on the screen: a man probably ten or fifteen years older than he is, and a child, baby hair almost white and sparse, gummy grin. He sets the phone down between them and puts both hands on the wheel. Brendan is only a little older. A year, maybe. He glances at the woman, and his heart pulls so many ways he can't name one of them. She is pretty, but that's all she has in common with her. He swallows something, thinks of the park a couple years ago. They pass a gas station and a library on the left, an older woman salting the walkway. The light is up ahead, and it turns red and he stops. A couple cars pull up on the other side, and he wonders if they can see into the truck, see her slouched there. The light is still red, and no one is coming. He lets off the brake and drives through the light, and the silver flank of a semi fills his rearview. The firehouse is right there, and his arms and legs feel heavy getting out and running to the door. The reception area is vacant, two chairs, a gumball machine. There's a glass booth set into the wall with no one in it, and he realizes he should have called on the way. A payphone sits off to one side, and he fishes for a quarter and dials 911. Dispatch picks up on the second ring. He paces as close to the door as he can get, looks out at his truck and at the woman inside.

 I just freaked out, he says. I saw her and didn't know what to do. He is flushed suddenly and, after hanging up, walks outside. It is as though he has killed her, as though he wrecked her car. He feels like he has left something important behind.

 He gives the medics a fake name, and they are satisfied. They pull her out of the truck and straight onto the gurney, load her into the back of the ambulance, and leave him there on the street with their lights going and the siren, and he watches the red flash over the sides of the houses as they drive away. He wanted to ask about her, to follow them to the hospital, but instead he gets into the truck and pulls a U-ey to head back the way he came.

 It's 3:56 by the clock, and the sun is heading down. In another hour, the snow will be blue and the stars will come out and Brendan will be at the door, breathing steam on the glass, drawing in it. He passes through the intersection and drives out of town, meets the start of traffic coming home and the end of it leaving for work. People going out for second shift at the Honda plant, a grind he could never take even if they'd hire him. Her phone lights up and bleats. He picks it up, puts it back. Turning down Lewis Road to make sure the Explorer is gone, he thinks he'll just chuck the phone out the window. But there's the truck, still. No rollback in sight. He parks the Ranger and gets out, switches her phone for his, and calls MD.

 MD picks up on the first ring. Bryce, man, you're not gonna believe this shit.

 What, he says.

 Tranny dropped on that F600. Pull the usual offa the wreck. We're gonna have to let it go.

 He nearly sits down in the road. All right.

 Traffic on your woman is bad. They called her soon as they got her.

He nods. I figured.

Foulk's Towing on its way. You probably got half an hour. Sheriffs are tied up across the county.

He's silent for a minute, stuck between the two trucks. He turns back to his.

Well, see you back here.

Yeah. He hangs up. He puts his phone away thinking of the double-wide, dark and dry from the plug-in heaters, his son's chapped nostrils, him tugging on the cord of the phone while Grandma stands beside him, waiting, too. As he gets his tools from the bed of the truck, he thinks of the baby on the woman's phone, and the man, the husband. He wants to call MD to see if there was traffic about contacting family, but they probably asked off-air.

He takes a tarp and his toolbox from the back, throws the tarp down below the Explorer, and slings himself under the truck, eases to the back of the engine block. He looks along the exhaust and raises the screwdriver up to the first O2 sensor to peel back the plastic and stops. What was above him, what was warm and like a home, maybe, this truck. He thinks of sitting in the backseat, looking at the mom and dad, holding hands between the seats, or her hand on his thigh. All the things he didn't get to do, won't, the things Brendan will never see. And if he does, they won't be right. They won't be like this kid saw. It won't be his mother.

The first sensor comes off easy, and so do the rest. Scooting himself out from under the wreck, he feels the cold seep in from the ground below. He stands and opens the passenger door to lean over and flip the lock on the hood and something pale catches his eye in the backseat. He looks ahead, through the cracked windshield, and moves to shut the door. His feet slip out, and he sits down against the tire. A semi or two passes along the highway.

The field across the way looks barren. Like nothing could grow there, like the rows of stover are all there ever was, jagged above the snow. Again he thinks, I could go. Try again tomorrow. This is only his third week. But he's already seen this, and he thinks the driver heading this way doesn't need to. So he calls 911 from his phone. He says he just came up on a wreck and the dispatcher tries to tell him it's taken care of, and he says, No. No, it's not. He says, There's a kid here in the back, and the woman on the other end goes quiet. She finally asks his name, and he gives it. Then she asks him to wait there for the deputy or the ambulance, and he says, Yeah, I'll wait. She wants to keep him on the line, but he says, I'll wait, again and hangs up.

He stands and walks into the field, following the tracks, and he takes out the woman's phone. There are five missed calls and a couple text messages, and he clears the notices to see the picture again, but the background is of flowers. He bends down to set the phone in the snow, and walks back to his truck, hands deep in his pockets for the cold and the shivering.

Miss Valley City, North Dakota

Charles P. Ries

It was an odd place to be a beauty queen,
butt square in the middle of America.
Where drinking, eating red meat,
and killing time outside Woolworth's
was considered gainful employment.

A Great Plains beauty with a lost look
from a past life that told you she
wasn't comfortable wearing this town's
tiara. Wondering why any thinking God
would reenter her *here*. In this place,
to eat buffalo burgers and to be confused
with someone else. Making amends for
past life sins.

Maybe this is why she tried to drink her
brains out. Pounding away her sense of
strangeness to make her soul fit here, but
drunk or not, they loved her and voted
her their Queen of Valley Days in 1972.

They wrapped their beauty queen's
head in a garland of Prairie Chicken
grass, gave her a scepter of wheat
husks, circled her ivory porcelain
neck with a string of Swedish meatballs,
and carried her down Main Street in a
white Chevy convertible chariot.

Years later, after she dried out, moved
away, began to live in real time and
remember her days, she made friends
with life and walked the middle road
between drunks and born-again Christians.
She discovered she could zap pain
away with a flick of her forefinger.
She liked doing this better than
drinking and began to live dangerously.

In time, she yearned to return to
that white convertible and smell
it all over again. To see it with
young, sober eyes at middle age.
The people outside Woolworth's
were glad to see her. Pleased to
have her flick her finger their way.
She would always be Miss Valley
City. And she came to know that
family is family, and the glue that
binds us together is greater than
the things that make us change.

VII.
(THE LEVIATHAN)

Mary Buchinger

She studies the leviathan

      learns every
            everlasting detail
each mole and dimple, curve of tooth

by heart—

      his physiognomy
            so much more
   familiar
to her
    than to himself.

   How he shifts in the company of others

  the ripple
       of self-consciousness
    the tics
      she cannot but love

only because she alone
        has paid attention

  and this makes him hers.

This knowledge, heart's sustenance,
    harvested
        like pomegranates
          —that honeycombed
            and jeweled fruit
       of banishment,
          fertility, promise—

    knowledge unwrapped and crushed, juices
      staining her fingers, wrists, arms.

This, the myth she was handed.

    Devouring, bit by bit, what one has grown to love—

        this, love's requirement.

The Poor Man's Guide to an Affordable, Painless Suicide

Schuler Benson

Dean flips off that switch in himself as the mom pulls her dead infant from its casket in the middle of "Bridge Over Troubled Water." I grasp at the version of that switch in myself, a lack that is not yet absence. Manning my place in the back right corner of the funeral home's tent, I'm cut in half by sunlight, standing next to the speakers I usually have on my office desk. We of the death business are the standard-bearers of gallows humor in this life, and Dean joked earlier about me taking a break from being a peckerwood to emcee this party as "DJ Peckerwood." We never laugh, but recollect it.

This mother coddles a limp baby boy, her hands hooked into claws, squeezed so tight around the corpse that I reckon something's bound to pop. For the first time in months, I feel my gut twist in prep to retch, and I turn my face away. Methodists in attendance restrain the mom, and Mr. Pierce from the funeral home pulls the baby from her. He places it back in its casket, tucking it in as if he were folding clothes, and shutting the lid like he'd close the cover of a wake registry. I make myself small beneath the bedlam and creep away, cemetery mud like shit icing around the edges of my loafers, to where Dean stands by the backhoe.

"Why you green, nigga?" he says, lighting a cigarette. "Ain't nevah seen a baby doll?"

The mom is among the last to leave when the service ends, carried wounded-soldier style to a waiting limousine, limp as Christ hung between two human crutches. The car stutters off, and I ease into my walk back to the office across the street, through new November. Behind me, I hear Dean firing up the backhoe to plow through the same slop that clutches at my heels. The mud here is loath to let anything go. It sucks against my soles and sounds like Peter used to when he'd squirt a stream of snotty spit from the gap between his front teeth, before time and braces drew it shut, then slurp it back up just before it touched grass, snapping back like a bad tendon and slathering his mouth with sheen.

I reach the office, go inside. On my desk, Angie's left a memo that reads "Moslium Smell." I have no fresh ideas. And I cannot process the problem with the scent of the place. We fill it and fill it with dead folks, and it just keeps smelling like pine oil. People complain about anything.

Sitting down behind my desk, I fold Angie's note into tinier and tinier squares as I look at my wall calendar. I've never had a job with vacation time before this one, and as of next week, I'll have three days to go upstate to the nursing home and watch Mason while he lies in bed on a vent. I'll bring pictures of the women, pictures of Mom and Peter, and I'll post them up around his bed to remind him of them and us and me, and why I keep him there and keep him alive, and I'll smuggle in his favorite foods in Ziplocs and little Gladware containers and eat them at his bedside. I'll wipe my hands and mouth on his sheets. I'll know he'll know I'm there.

Mason's been in a vegetative state since a single-car accident eleven months ago. Insurance is incredible—take a dead man and keep him alive. But Mason had no people. No one but me. After nearly a year in a bed, dreaming awake, a brain wired to waste and stranded in life, Mason's insurance will no longer cover his convalescence. I'm taking vacation to watch him die.

Digger Dean is a hardass. He likes to say, "All my daddy ever gave me was a hard time and some Camel Cash at Christmas." He smokes, haloed by waning sunlight, as I trudge through 4C to where he leans waiting by the backhoe. The text he sent me read: "kum kwik when u can." As I approach Dean, the backhoe, and an open grave, he looks at me like he's the kid who brought his big sister's dildo to school.

"You ever seen a muthafuckin' skull?" his words hula-hooping smoke rings.

I light a cigarette of my own.

Before a headstone marked ERWIN, is the grave Dean's been digging for the last half hour. It is approximately eight feet deep, and the bottom foot is filled with black sludge, punctuated by jutting pieces of rotten wood. What floats in the grave appears to be part of a pinstripe-suited shoulder, the toe of a withered leather shoe, and, indeed, a human skull.

In 1988, the city passed an ordinance mandating all human remains interred in earthen graves within the town limits be placed inside a casket, and that the casket be sealed within a vault made of concrete, steel, or polypropylene. Anyone buried before that was subject to The Shift. The earth has a way of sending things back up. Plant seeds; crops grow. It's natural for what's buried to find its way to the surface, or at least to make a move elsewhere. In the business, The Shift is older guys' name for soil creep: when layers of dirt and clay above bedrock move beneath the landscape. If there's something foreign down there, it moves, too. Ezra Erwin was interred in 1967. His wife, Magda, died three days ago. Dean came out to dig a hole for Magda, and Ezra saw sunlight for the first time in decades.

"This ever happen before?"

"Naw, not since I been workin'," Dean says.

"So, what's the plan?"

"Angie still in Shreveport?"

"Yeah, 'til next week."

"Arrite, I don't see why nobody but us gotta know," he says. Dean flicks the butt of his Salem into the stew with the earthly remains of Ezra Erwin and climbs onto the digger. As I step away from the yawning, muddy rectangle, the arm of Dean's backhoe moves its shovel over the grave, where it hovers momentarily.

"*Liiike a briiiiiidge oh-vaaah tuh-rubbled waahtaaaah*," Dean sings, as he plunges the machine into the ground. The arm shudders, crushing Erwin's skeleton into the ten- or eleven-foot range, a depth unfamiliar with digesting the dead. We never even knew this man to violate him so. "That's what they call a 'essecutive decision.' They woulda just laid side-buh-side fuh all time," Dean drawls, shutting off the ignition. "Now she jus' gon' be on top. I like to think they like that."

Our mom and Mason tied the knot when we were kids. He signed the paperwork on Peter and me not too long after. Mason was a counselor at the mental health and drug rehab center where Mom dried out, and the shelves in his office were filled with little wooden animals he'd carved from cedar blocks. Peter and I could never figure out what kind of animals they were. Pigdogs. Sickly buffalo. An ostrich or the Loch Ness Monster. A two-headed man. Mason dipped three cans of Skoal a day, and he was the ugliest man I'd ever seen. He tried to tell us about what he called the "sunlight of the spirit," this thing he said guided him, led him to us. Peter and I thought it sounded like something from *Heebie Jeebies*, that fake *Goosebumps* series they had at book fairs. A ghost story eaten and thrown back up. What guided Mason didn't feel like sunlight.

Before he married Mom, Mason took us camping at a scout camp near the Louisiana line, while Mom went to the Tunica boats with the woman who cut her hair. We didn't think anything of it when he drove his truck through a ditch around the locked gate to the camp. We set up in one of the sites near the main dirt road that ran beside the mess hall and trading post. Mason said we were roughing it, so Peter and I were excited when we found toilet paper left in the site latrine by whoever had camped there earlier in the summer. The second day, cooking in humidity and bored as hell while Mason traded off whittling on little critters and sticks, we took one of the rolls from beside the jagged hole in the latrine's wooden bench, and we pulled pieces of tissue off, threw them at each other, made spitballs. Laughed, fell down, rolled around, got dirty. Neither of us noticed Mason walking over, creeping like he did.

"Why make a mess?" he said.

I didn't answer. Peter sneezed. Mason folded up his whittling knife and put it in his pocket, then ran his thumb along an oak branch he'd been balding. I felt the sting of it on my cheek before I even knew he'd swung it. I grabbed my mouth, fell down, too shocked to cry.

"Why make a mess?"

Peter's shot at running was broken by the belt loop Mason hooked with two fingers. He put the cane twice to Peter's ass, then threw him into the dirt beside me.

"You boys," Mason said, twirling his stick. "You're gonna clean up every shred of this. You're gonna fix it. Every bit." He wedged the stick beneath his armpit and dropped his hands to his crotch, pulling down his zipper as he sauntered a few feet from us to one of the biggest piles of toilet paper. "Every bit," he repeated, over the sound of piss hitting dirt with the same *thop* the hose made when we'd drink from it during halftime in sandlot.

"No," Peter said.

"'Scuse me?"

"No. *No.* I am not touching that. I'm *not* touching *that* after you ... after you *pissed!*"

As Peter pulled his knees beneath him to stand, Mason lurched forward, fly gaping, and brought his stick down again, squarely to the top of Peter's head.

"Accountability," he spat over Peter's sobs. "Accountability and respect, boys. God frames everything we do." He two-handed the stick and slammed it down over his knee, snapping it in half. Mason walked back to the pile of pissy toilet paper and clutched a dripping gob of it between the two halves. "Use tools," he said, dropping the sticks between where Peter and I lay. He zipped his fly as he walked back toward our folding chairs sitting around firewood we never lit.

Mom tied the noose when we were seventeen. We didn't know why then, but we found out later when Mason was fired from the center. Four women came forward and accused Mason of raping them while they were under his care between 1991 and 1998. Then two more. Then another. All those women, all those pointed fingers, and still there wasn't enough evidence for Mason to have to do any time. I wanted them to come together, to hold each other's hearts, swarm on him, and pick his bones. But the center just fired him, and he moved. Peter and I lived with our grandmother until we turned eighteen, then got a place of our own. I didn't hear about Mason again until a cop called to tell me about his wreck. Peter moved off the day before our twenty-first birthday. He never said bye. Just left a note that he was going to do rig work offshore.

Peter and I played this game when we were little. At the house Mom moved us into when she married Mason, was a round coffee table with a glass top. We'd sit across that table from each other and run our tongues along the glass edge, crawling, hands and knees, around the circle. Friction sliced a wet notch in the tip of my tongue, but I kept going. Around and around, the taste of my blood. Peter's spit. Peter's blood. From the open window, we could hear the trailer girls singing while they swung jumpropes and scratched nubs of chalk on broken concrete:

The widow in the field
Got a fortune, I'm told
Off a brine pit 'n forty foot'a copper she sold
Fly me away
Pretty silver and gold
To a beach down south where it never gets cold.

We did it to see each other. Seeing Peter was always the same as looking in a mirror, but this way we were across from each other, eye to eye, with our own reflections haunting the periphery, swimming on smoky glass and warping into one another at the center of the table's concave bowl. Two copied heads fading into one at the hairline. A two-bodied boy.

Jeb is the owner, and he's in town the day the Winstons come to talk about a plot for Allen, their newly dead patriarch. Jeb owns this land from two thousand miles away. Today, he's here inspecting the grounds, and decides he'll show me how it's done with the Winstons. My numbers are low lately. People have to buy plots, but I'm failing on selling stones. They're going to Anson Monuments down the road. In the business of eternity, there's a quota to meet.

"Well, he had insurance, but it don't pay out for what he done," Charlie Winston says. "Don't know what to do 'bout a coffin or sprays or nothin'. We still got a lot to work through on Daddy's affairs."

"I see," Jeb says.

He sits at my desk. I stand behind him. The placard in front of my PC monitor is engraved with my name, and "Funeral Services Counselor" beneath it. When I ordered it, I requested the trophy shop use Papyrus font.

"Typically, these arrangements are made with the funeral homes, and we just handle the interment," Jeb states. Tendons, or wires, as the man may be a goddamn robot, shimmy between his jaw and neck as he speaks and thinks. He is a man who talks to things, who is here to deal with his property and scores of numbers that represent money and customers and the dead.

"Right," Charlie mutters. His mother grunts in her Rascal chair next to him. "Well. I got Daddy's checkbook right here. Mr. Pierce can't sit down with us 'til Monday. Since insurance don't pay out, we just rather cut a check now for the plot before a buncha bills come due."

"Section G is prime real estate," Jeb says, no hesitation.

The mother whinnies, clicks her teeth, chews the inside of her cheek. Her eyes roll like rounded dice. Her wheelchair whines a mosquito tone probably only I can hear.

"Y'all got any kinda specials or sump'm? Like a three-fer-one or two-fers or nothin'?" Charlie says.

"You'd like a three-space plot in Section G?"

"Yeah, all together."

"In purchases of two spaces or more, rates per space drop to twenty-four hundred," Jeb calculates.

I cough. The mother smells a fart.

"Godamighty," Charlie sighs. "All right, what's the math on that?"

"Altogether, for the three-space plot in Section G, the going total is seven thousand, two hundred dollars."

"Christ Jesus," Charlie spits as he scribbles on his daddy's last check.

Jeb takes the check and places it in an envelope inside the family's new file. Charlie stands, his mother fiddles with her joystick, and they leave our building in staggers and hums. No handshakes.

"Plots are twenty-two hundred one at a time in G," I tell Jeb.

"This isn't a potter's field," he counters. "He pulled out a dead man's checkbook." Jeb rearranges the shit on my desk, and then gets up to go inspect the mausoleum. "You guys' digger talks like he's black."

"Yeah," I say.

"Don't let him talk to anyone who matters," he trails, as he exits.

Apart from the neck wires, most of the rest of Jeb is unassuming, except for his forearms. Those fucking forearms make him even more of a caricature. Massive, illusory, beneath the static of swarming, salt-and-pepper yeti arm hair that coats them like shredded fiberglass insulation. I hate Jeb. I hope he dies on his own property so we can feed him to it. I leave my office and walk out the back way, through the garage, to smoke.

We are the worst people, providers in reverse. I cut on the light in the garage and survey my hands, thinking of the store I worked at before I came to the cemetery. Stocking shelves laid my cuticles to shreds every day from full shifts of tearing cardboard, blood drying brown, muddying with glue and tiny paper splinters. By the end of each day, my fingers were filthy little medusas, and I couldn't tell what was me and what was packaging. At night when I come home from the cemetery now, I miss digging the grime out from under my nails. It hurt. I miss cleaning that squalor of money pulled from beneath a flopped tit, bathroom keys attached to broken wooden rulers, handed back to me wet. When I was done with my hands, they were ugly, but they were clean.

After raising the garage door, I hear voices. Charlie and Dean talk, while some woman who stayed in the van helps Mrs. Winston and her wheels onto a lift. I lean against the garage door track, smoking, and I listen to Dean and Charlie.

"Too goddamn broke to die," Charlie swears.

"Mmm hmm," Dean mumbles.

"You go to March Hill?"

"Yeah," Dean says. "We people. You was '95, right?"

"Yeah."

"Ninety-nine," Dean says.

"Right, right."

"This 'boutcho daddy?"

"Yeah. Blew 'is goddamn head off."

"God damn."

"Yep."

"Give 'emm troubles to the Man," Dean says. I hear the butt of his cigarette smack against the decorative plastic flowerpot we use as an ashtray, parking lot gravel chuckling beneath his feet as he heads toward the backhoe.

"Uh, Mr. Winston," I fumble, moving too fast, popping out like a jack-in-the-box.

He spins around. "Huh?"

"I, uh. I just wanted to apologize for my boss," I stutter, rubbery, talking with my hands. "He's a numbers guy, you know? He's not good at this part."

Charlie grunts.

"Look. Can I, uh ... I'm sorry, can I ask you something?"

He looks over to the lady helping his mother. The two women are wrapped in an awkward dance. On the platform, off the platform, whirring, buzzing. Grunts and clicks. Charlie lights a new cigarette with the butt of the one he just finished.

"Shoot."

"You say," I hesitate, "you say he shot himself?"

"Yeah."

"What, uh ... what—"

"It don't matter," he cuts me short. "I seen it comin', and I let it happen. He was a sad ole fuck, and it was either that or just keep livin' and let cancer do it. Woulda ended up in hell, either way."

I burn another nail, pause, and watch the women. "You believe in hell?" I ask, looking at the tip of my smoke.

"I wanted to when I thought I had somebody to send there." He pauses. "Now, I think it's just, uh ... endings."

Whirring, buzzing.

"Daddy got his," he says, blowing smoke and words. "Standin' here now, though, I don't think it woulda mattered how he got that end. All I care is he got it. Now, I can live 'til I get mine."

"What'll you do?"

"Just wait, I s'pose." He puffs, throwing his mostly unsmoked cigarette into the ashtray. He shoves his hands into his pockets, keeps watching his mother and the woman. "We found 'im out back the house. He'd been fuckin' around out there last three, four months, doin' we didn't know what. I seen when I found 'im. He'd been fixin' up this old johnboat."

I put out my cigarette. His mother finally situated in the van, Charlie makes his way toward the passenger side door as the woman cranks the ignition.

"Maybe I'll work on the boat while I wait," he says. "Only thing he ever tried to fix."

When we were 22, Peter faced me from across the round, glasstop table in the den of my apartment. I hadn't seen him in a year. His face was some kind of soft death mask that looked like mine, but he didn't look grim at all. We got frown lines early, and his looked shallow. I thought maybe it was relief.

His head lay on its side by the tray where my remotes sat, lips blue, eyes glassy and glazed over but still fixed on the rig and baggie in front of him. He did it while I was at work. I got home to find him in my den, blue and white as a flag, body draped limp like one. I walked up slowly, sliding out of my loafers and dropping my blazer to the ground behind me. I knelt on my side of the table, eyes level with his. Leaned forward, stuck my tongue out. I pulled back, dug out my phone. Called 911. Waited, cried, and tried to unsee what I'd look like dead. My table reflected nothing.

Pierce's calls me at work the day before I plan to head up north, and they say to expect a family for a service Tuesday. They're on their way to me now. Mr. Pierce tells me he put in a good word for me on our marker rates. I thank him and hang up the cordless, which slips out of its dock and rolls beneath my desk. I chase the phone down there and don't want to get up. On the underside of the center drawer, I notice "lol this is hell lol" carved into the aluminum.

At the back of the cemetery is a section we don't use. It's a geological anomaly. A bottomless pit. The place became a cemetery when the owner had this plot of land consecrated in the late 1800s after he realized there was nothing else he could do with it. The pine that grew on the south side was diseased. It still is. They didn't look for oil after sounding the pit and finding out they had no idea how far back it reached underneath them. Various owners of the cemetery have had plenty of trouble from it over the years, running off kids who come to drink or fuck, people who ask if they can throw trash in it, rednecks who kill deer out of season and come in through the woods on four-wheelers to dispose of the carcasses someplace secret. Some drunk fell into it in the eighties. They never recovered his body. I heard once that a local Indian tribe believed the first people crawled out of the ground at the beginning of time, born of mud by a loving mother. They came from beneath the earth. I wonder if this is their hole. Why they'd climb out of it. Why they'd leave the womb.

Beneath the desk, I feel like I'm back in the womb, but alone this time, and I am both comforted and horrified. For the first time since I saw him dead, I think I miss Peter, and dread rises in me, quick and pure, and I can't shake the thought of whether or not there's anything left in this life that he fixed.

I scramble out from beneath my desk, out of the womb, out of the office and into my car, ducking out on the Pierce referral. Half an hour later, I exit the storage unit where I put Mason's shit. I leave the unit key in its lock, and just before the door slams shut, I flick in Angie's mausoleum memo, the only piece of paper I could find in my blazer pocket. On the back of her note, I'd written: "TO AUCTION." Then, I go home and think and eat and sleep. The next morning, I drive to the place where Mason waits.

"You're the stepson, right?"

"Yes," I say.

"In Mr. Becker's file, it says Nancy spoke with you last week, that you've been made aware of the full prognosis, lack of progress, the possibilities—"

"Yes. I spoke with Nancy. I understand."

"I see. Pastor Holland, our chaplain, has made himself available—"

"I don't need a pastor; thank you."

"I, uh," she falters.

I try to smile at her.

"The doctor will be down shortly. As per guidelines, everything is documented. It's very clean. Very peaceful. If you'd like, you can have a seat here in the lobby."

"Would you mind—" I start. "Can I see him?"

Mason doesn't look evil anymore. He doesn't look scary. He's small and feeble, gnarled and frail. Bones, cords, and tubes beneath a sheet, an accordion in a ribcage. A carcass disposed of someplace secret. He's still so ugly. I feel my gut twist in prep to retch and start to turn my face away, but I stop. I stop and look, look at him. Across his room, the shades are drawn. I am cut in half by sunlight.

"It's clear now, Mason," I say. "It's all clear. Can you see it? God frames everything I do, Mason. With tools. Can you see?"

I pull his old whittling knife from my pocket, click it open slowly. The skin of my face shakes as my skull vibrates.

"You're a dried-up piece of shit before me, and I've been given by God the tools for your disposal. I won't even have to touch you. I won't have to get your shit on me."

I drag the blade beneath my nails.

"You're human shit. You're shit, Mason. See? You're shit, and I stay clean."

Get all that dirt out.

"Bright and clean in the sunlight of the spirit."

I close the knife and lay it longways on his chest. Rise. Fall.

"Mason," I choke, clear my throat. "Mason. Mason. You can go now."

The administration woman from the lobby sees me leaving Mason's room.

"Sir, the doctor's headed this way. Sir. Sir?"

I walk and keep walking, down the hall, through the lobby. Out the front door. Into the light.

Back at work, my face in December wind, I look out across the cemetery. I straighten my tie, button the cuffs that will collar the hands that will shake the hands of the bereaved and take their money and bury their dead. Sway in the shoes that will carry me over dirt for sale, through this life that may, or may not, be a wet bathroom key. While I wait with men on hollow earth, wait to fill it. While I wait and wonder what, if anything, I can fix. From my inside coat pocket, I produce a new lockblade. From my slacks, a small, rounded knob of cedar. I cut at the stem that tapers down from its end, a knotty nub slowly beginning to take the shape of a hoof. Breeze picks up, moves me, and my blazer billows out behind me like a flag. This ground is loath to let anything go, but it feels like a strong enough gust could pry me loose. Fly me away. Somewhere further south. Somewhere offshore.

WILLIAM BARRET QUESTION MARK

CEE

Am I a pseudo-British, condescending asshole
Who could kick champion ass in World Fencing?
Do I strut and sneer and bite out my bitterness
"How *USELESS!!, Sen—nor Seg—guin ... !*"
Do I, indeed, think my shit don't stink?
Am I a pale, should-have-played-for-Marilyn-Manson, pseudo-Goth
Who's swallowed up by 'ee's mini-Mad Hatter hat?
Do I mumble and murmur and give the impression
That I not only don't think my shit don't stink,
I don't even think I could get it up?

I think I'm neither
I think I'm a man you never knew, nor ever, ever will
Who never saw the bullet coming
Even though I'd seen it clear, there, in the air
Hovering, for thirteen days

THE THING IS, YOU SEE

Normal

god has big eyes &
he puts them in the mouths
of little children &
you can do what you will
with a child, but
one way or
another
what you will
will come back to speak
to you
when you are old
when your hands are
arthritic
when your knees
buckle
when your mind is
growing thin, (oh yes)
that tiny voice
will speak &
speak &
speak

Kinda Sorta American Dream

Steve Karas

I'm in the supper line behind fifty white-bearded fat asses ready to stack my plate high with fried chicken, buttered egg noodles, and creamy cabbage salad. Might as well get something out of this. "Welcome Class of 2012" is spelled out above the dinner choices on the menu board. When we graduate—those of us who do—we'll be the seventy-fifth group to stake that claim. I didn't get into Harvard, and I've never been much of a Christmas guy. In fact, I dropped out of community college after a year and always preferred Halloween, so the fact that I'm here, at the Harvard of Santa schools, so they say, makes it plain just how twisted life is.

I find a seat at an empty table, bread buns rolling off my plate like snowballs.

"Sit over here, pal," one of the Santas calls out to me.

"Saved this spot for you."

"Come on, join us!"

It's amazing how much friendliness is exaggerated here.

"Thanks, fellas," I say.

For a lot of these guys, this isn't their first rodeo. Unlike me, most are retired and have been playing Santa for years to make a little extra income. I'm sandwiched between an ex-land surveyor and an aerospace engineer. An agricultural salesman is slurping down a casserole right in my face. Some of these guys have been here before and are signed on for a tune-up, you know, to work on the ho-ho-ho or pick up new tips on beard grooming. One Santa—Gill—is already getting on my last nerve. He's Southern-California-tan, bragging to us about how he doesn't need the money, how he volunteers his time at hospitals and village tree lightings. I want to reach across the table and smack him upside the head with a drumstick.

From the windows, we can see flakes beginning to fall. Gill, of course, breaks out into song—"Let It Snow"—and pretty soon the whole cafeteria is rockin'. I feel like quite the imposter because, I'm embarrassed to admit, I don't even remember the words. I'm no Santa. At six-four, a hundred ninety pounds wet, I look more like Frankenstein than anything. I scan the room, move my lips, bounce my head anyway. I do my best to stumble through it without letting on how lost I am.

"I don't feel comfortable here," I tell Barb.

We're in our dorm room. She doesn't respond or even look up, just keeps unpacking her suitcase and putting clothes in drawers. Her not saying anything says a lot. Like, *Well, you better suck it up, Wayne, unless you got a better idea because, as of now, we've run out of options.*

"Mom paid," she finally says, "and we're already here."

My mother-in-law, The Meddler, saw a segment about this place on 20/20. Since I've been out of work awhile, she forked out the cash for this mini-camp and sent us as an "early Christmas gift." In three days I'm supposed to be miraculously transformed into Santa, and Barb into Mrs. Claus. The Meddler said it would give us the chance to find seasonal work, and when she said it, I could tell she thought of herself as quite the do-gooder, which royally pissed me off. But Barb decided it might be a good idea for us to give this a try, and I'm in no position to argue with her.

"I'm going to call and see how the boys are doing," Barb says, her hair dyed white and pulled up into a bun, which is still wigging me out.

Before the plant shut down almost a year ago, we paid our mortgage on time for a nice ranch outside Detroit. Barb stayed home with the boys —now fourteen, eleven, and six—and I made a modest living. We'd take summer camping trips to Muskegon or Ossineke, had even been to Canada once. We were kinda sorta living the American Dream. The boys haven't wanted much to do with me in my recent mood state and now they're crashing with their grandpa and The Meddler, who I'm sure are doing their best to convince them they're better caretakers than us.

"Do you want to say goodnight to Dad?" Barb says. "Boys? Oh, hey, Mom. Where'd they go?" She glances at me and shrugs.

"Guess not," I mumble.

The room smells like peppermint. Coupled with the Christmas decorations it's smothered in—a candy cane bedspread, creepy talking Santa doll, wooden nutcrackers—I feel nauseous, like I've eaten too much candy. Even though I know it's probably not for the best, I wish I were back in the comforts of my own home. I wish I were alone in my den, where I feel safe at least, searching for jobs that don't exist or that I'm not qualified for, obsessively checking my family's online bank account, watching our savings slowly disappear.

It's the ass crack of dawn, the dean of the school is at the podium in the front of the great hall (interestingly, the only guy in here with a clean shave), and I'm sipping on burnt coffee out of a Styrofoam cup. I can't stop scratching my neck because my newly dyed beard, only three-weeks' growth at this point, is itching to no end. I flip through the schedule: nonstop sessions on marketing and promotion, fitness training, and posing techniques, to name a few. On the last page, I read "Final Test (Hint: In Front of TV Cameras)" and my stomach churns.

"Kids expect perfection," the dean says. "That means you need to have fresh-smelling breath, know all the reindeer names, act like you've lived in the North Pole your whole life. And it helps to have real reindeer doo doo on the soles of your shoes."

The Santas laugh in unison—a hearty laughter that rumbles from deep within their bowels. The white Santas, the Latino Santas, the one black Santa, even. I'm having a hard time understanding what's so funny, especially at the crack of dawn's ass.

"Give it your all on every effort," the dean continues, "because each kid will remember you forever. To be a great Santa, you have to want to be him, embody his spirit, be willing to stay in character through highs and lows. I'm a firm believer you don't choose to be Santa; you're chosen to be."

I roll my eyes and search the crowd for someone sharing my skepticism—maybe a raised eyebrow, folded arms—but the rest of these suckers are all nodding their heads in agreement, hands on bellies.

"Enough from me," the dean says. "Let's go around and have each of you share your name and your wildest Christmas story."

As if a switch is turned on, my heart begins hammering away at my chest cavity, and I know where this is going, so I bail. I mutter something to the Santa next to me about having to hit the head, though I really don't care if he hears. Barb is running late to her Mrs. Claus meeting and is still in our room, slipping into her plaid worsted cloak. She looks like Mrs. Doubtfire, and that actually calms me a bit.

"I can't do this," I say. "I'm freaking out. They're having us get up and talk about ourselves and we're supposed to be all cool and jolly."

"Why don't you take one of your Xanax, Wayne? Did you take your Xanax?"

"I hate having to rely on that stuff." I shake one out from the pill container anyway and fire it down my throat.

"You'll be fine," Barb says as she squeezes her hooves into black pointed shoes with fancy gold buckles we're supposed to presume were fashioned by elves. She stopped comforting me during these episodes months ago, and I'm not sure if she's just fed up or if it's tough love.

"All right, I guess I'll deal with it myself then," I say.

"Wayne, c'mon."

Six months back, I started waking up in the middle of the night scared I was about to die. The weirdest things are setting me off now on a regular basis. High school fears like speaking in public, talking to attractive ladies, calling about job openings.

I step closer to the door, and I can still hear Santas bellowing into the microphone: "Next thing I know my leg starts feeling wet and, sure enough, the kid's taking a leak on me!"

For some reason, I think of the boys, especially my fourteen-year-old, and I'm glad they're not here to see me pacing the room, shrinking behind the door. The schedule, rolled up in my fist, is tight enough to make a straw. I peer down at letters following the paper's curve, namely the letters "T" and "V." The boys would love to see their old man on the tube, wouldn't they? A younger version of me would have been the first to jump in front of television cameras and act a fool. I was the goof in the high school cafeteria doing magic tricks for crowds, making coins disappear in my hand, but now look at me. I crumple up the schedule into a furious little ball and dunk it into the snowman-shaped garbage bin.

―――

That afternoon, we're at a toy store in a local mall doing field research on the latest crazes: Furby, Elmo Live, something called a Lalaloopsy Silly Hair Star doll. Gill is examining a box holding a One Direction action figure. I believe it's Harry Styles, and I only know this because Barb says our fourteen-year-old is growing his hair out to look like him. He cares more about his Harry Styles hair, in fact, than about his grades, from what she tells me.

I see Gill nudge Barb, who's standing beside him. "One Direction?" he says. "Who are these guys? What happened to The Monkees and The Beatles, right? Now, those were bands." He cackles like it's the funniest thing he's said—ever—and Barb obliges him with a laugh herself.

I'm a few feet away, staring at a Ninjago Epic Battle Lego set, clawing at my beard, pretending not to pay any mind.

"Do you have any kids?" Gill asks her, this guy with his orange skin and white teeth, this George Hamilton in a Santa suit.

"Three," Barb says. "All boys."

"Three boys? You've got to be a saint, right? I'm in the presence of sainthood, and I don't mean Saint Nick. No offense to you, buddy," he says turning to me. Cackle, cackle. "How old are they?"

"The oldest is fourteen ..."

"There's no way you have a fourteen-year old. Get out! Even if you are supposed to be Mrs. Claus."

"I do, believe it or not. The next one is eleven and the youngest is—"

"Six," I interrupt. "The little guy's six."

Gill's eyes get wide as truck tires. He nods his head, giggles out of place, and goes back to fumbling with the Harry box. Barb pulls a doll from the shelf and clears her throat. She inadvertently presses its belly and the doll shouts, "I made a stinky!" I maneuver one of the little ninja Lego soldiers and poke his sword into the monstrous snake with its red eyes and silver fangs. Gill puts Harry away and moseys out of the aisle, beginning a carol under his breath.

―――

47

The next morning, the Santas are assembled in the great hall. The toy train is chugging its way around trays of pineapple and danishes. I'm downing my black coffee and eavesdropping on conversations. "How'd you get your beard to smell like a candy cane?" one Santa says to another. "Peppermint oil," the other one says. "That's my little secret." I roll my eyes. A 300-pound candy cane, all right.

The dean gets up to the podium and announces what's on tap for the day: dance lessons and sessions on liability insurance and makeup artistry. A child psychologist will be lecturing us, too.

"Before I send you off to your first session, let's talk about tomorrow's final project," the dean says. My chest tightens. "You've all been paired up and will take turns playing Santa at various locations across the area—daycare centers, old age homes, churches. Local newspaper and TV crews will be floating around to catch you in action."

That familiar feeling joins me as the Santas are bumping past to find out their assignments. I'm short of breath, and my mouth tastes like I'm sucking on batteries for mints. I'm caught in the stream of Santas, following the scent of peppermint and body odor, but inside I want to run. Inside, I'm a caveman with a sabertooth on his trail.

I don't even have the chance to open the card with my name on it and Gill's warm breath is heating my neck. "You're the only Wayne P., I take it, right?"

"Uh, yeah, I think so."

He extends his hand and grasps my sweaty palm. "Looks like it's you and me then, buddy. Our gig's at the Midland Mall. That's gotta be the primo assignment, right? Am I right?"

I stare at the raspberry jelly squeezing out of Gill's danish and onto his pearly whites. A Santa nudges my shoulder from behind and a speckle of coffee lands on my shirt.

"Whoa, you okay, buddy?" Gill says. "You don't look too good. Bleach in your beard getting to you?"

And then the music blares over the loudspeakers signaling us to move on to our first session of the day, and I'm off to the Rudolph Room to learn how to do the Christmas Waltz. Between Bing Crosby's "Silver Bells" and Gill's cackling, there's no time to think, and that's probably exactly what I need.

Barb and I are lying in bed watching the news. A blizzard is blowing in, they say. Over a foot of snow is expected to drop by tomorrow afternoon. Outside our window, things seem calm for now. A lamppost lights the mounds of snow, the lot of them glazed with a thin veil of ice, that have set up camp right there for the winter.

"Maybe they'll cancel this stupid final project," I say.

Barb doesn't look at me, only tucks her white locks behind her ears, pushes up her glasses with her trigger finger. "One more day, Wayne. And just think, once you have a diploma from here, you'll be like a Super Santa. You'll be able to work wherever you want, I bet."

"Super Santa. Fantastic, what I've always aspired to be. Maybe I can be like the jerkoff they've paired me up with."

"Oh, c'mon, Gill seems like a nice guy."

"He's not. But the good thing is, I'm sure his pompous ass will have no problem doing the whole gig on his own and I can sit back, blow smoke up his rear, and finish up so we can go home already."

"Maybe you should hang out with Gill, regain your confidence. It doesn't seem like anything bothers him. That's the way you used to be before all this."

This has an assortment of connotations and hangs in the air like god-awful breath. For ten years running, I was racking up World's Best Dad T-shirts and mugs each Christmas. Now whose fault is it I can't keep up the act? Whose fault is it I'm reduced to vying for the title of Super Santa?

"So, what," I say, "do you want to fuck the guy?"

Barb's head whips around and she glares at me, eyes crazy, mouth like a giant sinkhole.

"I'm sorry. That was dumb."

She jumps out of the bed. "What's wrong with you? Have you completely lost your mind?" She storms into the bathroom, slams the door, locks it. That doesn't stop her from yelling at me, though, and I'm a little embarrassed thinking if anyone hears us, it may dampen the Christmas cheer. "Now that your family needs you to step up," Barb says, "all you want to do is hide in your den like a damn groundhog waiting for the spring!"

"I'm sorry."

"I mean, what kind of man have you become?"

She keeps going like that for a while. Comments of that nature that slowly taper off. When she comes out an hour later, even after I say "sorry" for the umpteenth time, she doesn't make eye contact or respond. She gets into bed, and we're lying with our backs to each other. I can't sleep, and she periodically kicks the sheets and readjusts her pillow so I don't suppose she's sleeping much, either. I gaze out the window wondering how I let *this* go so far, and then snowflakes start to fall at some dreadful hour and I assume the blizzard has burst through the gates.

I'm the first Santa in the great hall. It's as quiet as this place has been, and even the Christmas lights haven't been turned on yet. The dean is getting the coffee brewed. I reach for a gingerbread scone from the breakfast table. "Is it okay if I grab one of these?"

"Oh, yeah, sure. Early bird gets the worm, right?"

I stare out at the snow falling down sideways, the wind combing the evergreens back like a big brush. The dean seems unfazed, goes back to the kitchen and brings out a fruit platter, like it's just another day in the

North Pole. I catch a glimpse of his Mrs. reaching for plates from a cabinet.

"So what line of work are you in back home," the dean says, "you know, when you're not donning the Santa costume?"

"I worked at a plant that manufactured parts for the auto companies. Drive-line parts mostly. Front and rear axles, propeller shafts. I was on the assembly line for seventeen years, but the plant closed down for good about a year ago. Been out of work since."

"Nothing else out there, huh?"

"Nothing else I know how to do."

"Well, you came to the right place."

"I suppose," I say.

"You got kids, Santa?"

"Three."

"Well, if there's any good in this, it's that you'll be able to relate as well as anyone when you have that sad little child on your lap asking you to get his daddy a job or help them keep their house."

A few groggy Santas, half-asleep, drag themselves into the hall. They nod their heads and mumble "Good morning" before lining up for coffee.

"Where you headed this afternoon?" the dean asks me.

"Midland Mall. With good ol' Gill."

"Oh, boy, guess you didn't hear. Gill went out skiing at Apple Mountain last night. Broke his leg. You won't be seeing him unless you plan on visiting the MidMichigan Medical Center."

"So what the hell does that mean for me?"

"I guess it means you're on your own, Santa. Think you can handle a mall full of overexcited kids?"

Fortunately, the mall is pretty much a straight shot down 10 because I'm on my own, and I can't see out of the windshield even with the wipers going full force. Barb is with the other ladies probably learning how to bake cookies, and even if she weren't, she wouldn't be with me. She hasn't talked to me since last night, and I'm sure she doesn't think I'd muster the balls to do this mall thing, which may very well be the reason I'm going.

With the snow, I'm expecting a light crowd, but of course it comes to a stop as soon as I get out of the truck. Because that's the twisted nature of this life. A plow is crashing through the lot, clearing the way for all the minivans and little tykes I imagine are eagerly throwing on their coats and boots in foyers across town. Inside, the mall is set for my arrival. In the center of the courtyard, behind kiosks selling chair massages and pillow pets, there's a towering tree with red and green ornaments. Beside it, there's a gold throne, my throne, surrounded by poinsettias and phony gift boxes. Carols are piping through the loud speakers: "You better watch out. You better not cry ..." It reminds me of a time not that long ago but that seems long ago, when I was the one on the other side of the red velvet rope with my three boys. To be honest, I don't even know if my six-year-old still believes in Santa.

I meet up with the general manager, a chubby fella with a five-o'clock shadow who looks like he could be a mall Santa, too, if he wasn't running this joint. He walks me into a back room, makes me sign some papers, and invites me to go ahead and get suited up. He wishes me a Merry Christmas in the same way a churchgoer would say, "Bless you, Father," to a priest, and then walks out.

I'm alone for the first time in full costume—suit, boots, hat, and gold-rimmed glasses. I examine myself in a smudged face mirror stuck to a file cabinet and realize it's been a while since I've done so. I don't look anything like me, but it is me. I don't think I look much like Santa, either, but as long as the kids buy what I'm selling, as long as one of them doesn't sniff me out, this can end up all right. I grab a Snickers from the vending machine and wolf it down for a little boost.

As I'm heading to my throne, I start feeling weak, hyperventilating. I try to remember everything I've absorbed over the last three days despite putting so much effort into not paying attention to any of it. "Keep your hands in plain view. Keep your hands in plain view. Keep your hands in plain view," I'm muttering under my breath. I give my mustache a little curl because it apparently gives more of a fantasy look, adds to the magic that is Santa. The line is building, I see, into a mass of moms and strollers, winter coats, and runny noses. The mall photographer is setting up, and I spot a TV crew lurking by the RadioShack. I can't feel my beard itch, and I'm not sure if that's a good thing.

My phone vibrates in my pocket, and I'm worried if someone sees me answering it I can get in trouble because maybe Santa isn't supposed to have a phone. But then again they're presumably making all these toys in the North Pole, right, so why wouldn't they have phones, too, in this day and age? Plus, it might be an emergency, so I pull it out. It's Barb.

"What's up?" I say. "I'm about to go on," thinking maybe she's calling to give me some last-minute moral support, declare how much she believes in me.

"I just had a call from my mom," she says. "Are you sitting?"

"Yes, I'm sitting. I'm sitting in my Santa throne."

"Your son decided to sneak out of the house last night. My parents found out when the police brought him home around midnight after they caught him drinking beer with two of his friends in an alley."

"You're telling me this now?"

My immediate reaction is to race out of here because I have a legitimate excuse. I'll do the three-hour drive home in two, grab my boy, and shake him. My boy whom I've barely spoken to the past six months, my boy who's growing his hair out to resemble a British pop star. As much as I'd like to ask him what he was thinking—*why?*—I know he won't have a good answer and I already kinda sorta know why, anyway. Besides, I have an army of toddlers that will hunt me down and trample me into the snow if I run for it at this point.

"I'm sorry I'm laying this on," Barb says. "I just had to tell you."

"I don't know what to say."

"Mom and Dad have been keeping an eye on him all day. We'll deal with this tonight. No point in leaving now, anyway, because we'll just get stuck on the highway with this snow."

"Ready, Santa?" the GM calls.

No, no, I'm not. But "Ho, ho" is what comes out of my mouth.

"Good luck," Barb says. "I'm proud of you, Wayne."

The first kid is being dragged toward me by his mom, and I don't have time to cry or yell or scrutinize my parenting. The kid is clinging to his mom as they near, terrified, like if he comes to me he'll be swallowed up into the abyss that is my fluffy red suit. The mom tries to drop him in my lap, but his arms are locked around her neck.

"It's okay, little pal. You can come here," I say.

"Oh, he did this last year, too," the mom says, swiping her dangling brown hair from her eyes.

Then why the hell did you bring him back? I'm thinking.

"Come on, sweetie," the mom pleads. "Santa just wants to know what you want for Christmas."

The kid is finally in my lap, but writhing, arching his back, one arm grasping his mom's top.

In a panic, I start thinking *WWGD—What Would Gill Do?* "Do you want to hear all about my reindeers?" I say. "Donner, Blitzer." But he doesn't stop thrashing. So I dig into my pocket and pull out a quarter. "Hey, hey, watch, little buddy. Watch what Santa can do."

He quiets a bit, his chest still heaving, though, snot running down his lip. He sneezes on me.

I show him the coin between my thumb and index finger. "Should we make it disappear?" I ask, and he nods. I swipe my right hand over the coin as if I'm grabbing it and then squeeze the hand shut. "Go ahead and blow on it," I say.

He looks to his mom for reassurance. "Blow on it, sweetie," she says, and so he does.

And then I slowly fan my fingers open for the big reveal and, lo and behold, the coin has vanished as far as the little guy can tell. His eyes widen, and it's the same expression my boys used to have when I would do the same trick for them. They'd gawk at me in amazement as if I were otherworldly, invincible, like they couldn't believe I was their dad. And I was pretty sure they'd never doubt me for a second.

By the time I make the coin reappear behind the kid's ear, he's not crying anymore. In fact, he's twiddling with my mustache. His mom backs away a few steps and the photographer snaps a picture I have to believe is a good one.

"Okay, so now let's get down to business, little man," I say. "What is it you want Santa to get you for Christmas?"

REIGN

Jared A. Carnie

I picked up a stick
And spiked the sky
Where the sparrows peered in.

I built my fortress.
I tested my troops.
I crushed my enemies. I worked tirelessly.
I was glorious.

Then Mum called "dinner"
From the back door
And the night destroyed my empire.

Sunrise Special

John Vicary

"You can't smoke that in here."

The old man peered over his glasses at the slip of a girl who'd interrupted his morning cigarette. "Since when?"

The waitress frowned. "Since always."

"That's not true. I've been coming here for years. And I always sit right here—right in this very spot—and have my cigarette." The old man held up his lighter, as if that provided proof.

"There are no-smoking laws in New York. I'm sorry, sir, but you'll have to go outside for that." The waitress sighed. Seven in the morning, and people were already giving her grief.

"Martha lets me," the man said.

"I'm not Martha."

The man snorted. "I noticed. Where is she?"

"I don't know. I'm here to take your order today. Can I bring you anything? Coffee?" She swirled the remains of a half-empty pot.

The man nodded. "Sure, sure. And lots of cream. Martha knows I like a lot of cream. I don't have to tell *her* that." As the waitress poured him his first cup, the man unfolded his newspaper. "So, I bet you hear a lot of things working here, am I right?"

"It's a diner, not a bar. Do you know what else you want, or do you need a minute?" The waitress tried not to tap her foot.

"Yeah, I'll have the Sunrise Special. So, no one ever tells you stuff, huh? What's your name, anyway?"

The waitress flicked her nametag. "How do you want your eggs?"

The man squinted. "Well, you're not much of a talker, are you? Agnes. What kind of a name is Agnes for a girl like you?"

Agnes shrugged. "I was named after my great aunt, you know? Eggs. How do you like them?"

The man smiled. "Sunny side up, Agnes. It suits you. I'm Howard. Nice to meet you."

"I'm glad you approve. That comes with toast. There's whole wheat, rye, sourdough, and white."

"Well, the kids these days and their names. It's good to hear something solid. Something you can wear for the rest of your life. Names are like coats, you know. You want to pick one that's going to last. Agnes will do you."

"Right. Well, my mom chose it, so next time she calls, I'll be sure to tell her thanks for giving me a coat name. Toast?"

"How come you aren't writing this down? How are you going to remember my order?" the man asked.

Agnes tried not to roll her eyes. "So far you haven't ordered, mister."

"Howard. Call me Howard."

"Can you just decide on the toast, or do you need a minute?" the waitress asked. Old people took forever and a day to do *anything*.

"You're in such a rush. It isn't like anyone else is even here. Rye, please. I'd like rye."

She nodded. "It comes with a side of meat. There's sausage links, patties, or turkey sausage. What will it be?"

"Do you ever want to tell a secret to someone who doesn't know you?"

"Why would I want to do that?" The waitress was too startled to bother with questions of meat. No one had ever asked her anything like that before.

He creased his paper between his fingers. "Sometimes it's easier to tell a stranger. That's all. Someone who doesn't know you might not judge you."

"That's silly," the waitress said, but as she said it, she didn't really think it was. It seemed to make perfect sense.

The man stared at her. "It's easy. I'll go first: I cheated on my wife."

"What?" Agnes set down the almost-empty coffee pot on the Formica table. "Why would you tell me that?"

"I needed to," the man said. "I had to tell someone. Your turn. Go ahead; it's amazingly cathartic."

Agnes swallowed. "You're crazy!" She didn't want to look at him, this old man in a buttoned-down shirt, sitting there calmly after he'd just admitted to cheating on his wife. It was surreal; that's what it was. People just didn't say things like that. "You're crazy." Then, she thought he must be going senile, and she felt bad for saying it twice.

"I'm a lot of things, but I'm not crazy." Howard tore open a tub of cream and stirred it into his coffee. "I loved my wife, you know. Very much. I'm not saying that to make myself sound better; if anything, that makes it worse. The thing is, she never knew I cheated. I'm so glad she never did. It would have hurt her so much. She's gone now, God rest her. But I had to tell someone, look someone in the face and admit that it happened. I mean, this was years ago. Years. Before you were a gleam in your mother's eye, as we used to say. I just had to tell someone and be free of it. And you're that someone, Agnes, so I thank you for that."

"But ... why?" The waitress sat down across from the man, even if it was against the rules. It felt silly to be looming over him, and besides, the diner really was empty. "Why did you?"

Howard sipped his coffee. "I've asked myself that so many times over the years, and every time I come up with a different answer. I don't know that there is any one reason. Certainly not one that you'll understand. I guess I just missed being in love. I didn't realize I had been all along."

The weight of his earnest admission hung in the air between them, a terrible imbalance, and she knew she had no obligation, but still, she wanted to tip the scale out of the valley of peculiarity they'd fallen into. "I never learned to tie my shoes," she blurted before she could stop herself.

The man blinked, his eyes owlish behind the trifocals.

Agnes held out her ankle, showing off the Velcroed shoe. "My parents weren't around much, and I just never learned when I should have. Then, I felt silly when I got too old, and I was embarrassed to ask. So that's it. My deep, dark secret."

"Feel better?"

She smiled. "Kind of, yeah." She stood. "I'll go place your order and bring you a refill on that coffee."

"I'd be most obliged, Agnes."

There was one other girl on the day shift, and Agnes motioned her over as she set another pot of coffee on to brew. "You see that guy in my section?" Agnes asked. "The old guy in the striped shirt?"

Heather nodded. "Howard? Yeah. He's a regular. Been coming for years. Why? He giving you trouble?"

"No, no. I was just wondering if he ever talked to you."

Heather shook her head. "Usually, he's in Martha's section. I've had him once or twice, but I don't think he's said anything to me. Did he say something nasty? Try to hit on you?"

"Ew. Heather. That's gross." Agnes wrinkled her nose. "He's nice. He's not like that."

Heather raised her eyebrows. "They're *all* like that, honey. You should know that by now."

Agnes made a face and took the man his refill. "Here's the cream. I didn't forget."

Howard lowered the paper he'd been reading. "I got arrested one time."

Her hand wavered, and she spilled a drop. "Excuse me?" Maybe Heather was right. Maybe it was indecent exposure.

"I've spent time in jail. You're looking at someone who has a misdemeanor on his record. I'm a criminal."

The waitress mopped up the spill with a rag from her apron pocket. "You don't seem like a hardened criminal," she said.

"I am."

"What did you do? Or is that the secret?" *Please don't be creepy,* she thought.

"I organized a strike. It turned ugly, and someone was hurt in the scramble that followed. Although, it isn't really a secret, I guess. It just bothers me; that's all. I never meant for anyone to be injured. If I could, I'd take it all back. That's something I regret, that people were hurt because of me. So, yeah, I'm a felon."

How could she have thought the worst of him? "Well, not in the strictest sense. A felon has a felony record. So you're not a felon ...

Howard."

He reached for his cup. "I guess you're as good'a waitress as Martha."

"Thanks." She scratched her forehead. "I had a baby." She tried not to cringe when she said it.

Howard set his cup down but said nothing.

Agnes kept talking, the words spilling out in a rush. "I was only sixteen, you know. Too young for a baby. They told me I could hold her, say goodbye, but I didn't want to. I know they thought I didn't care, and that bothered me. I *did* care. I did. I knew if I held her and smelled that baby smell, I'd never give her up. I moved up here the next summer, and I've never told anyone about that, never." She smoothed her apron. "Aren't you going to say anything? Aren't you going to say you're sorry or whatever it is people say? I always thought when I finally told someone that's what he'd say."

The man looked at her. "Do you want me to?"

"No. That's stupid." She wiped her eyes. "Why would you be? You don't even know me."

"I am sorry, but I wasn't going to say it. I think you're sorry enough. You don't need to hear it from a stranger. You just need to tell it. Have someone hear you." He tightened his mouth into a line.

"Yeah. Your food should be ready by now. I'll be right back." The waitress turned and marched to the counter. His Sunrise Special was the only one there, ready to be delivered. She picked it up and took it to him without further comment. She'd said enough already. God knows what Howard thought of her.

When it was time to bring him the bill, he cleared his throat. The waitress braced herself. He was probably going to say something, tell her how terrible she was, what an awful person—

"I'm dying."

Agnes blinked. "What?"

The man rolled the bill into a cylinder between his fingers as he talked. "I'm dying. I have cancer. It's these cigarettes—that's what they tell me. I guess it isn't a secret, my dying, but it was for a long time. This is my last day here, living my life the way I want to. My terms. My son is coming up from Georgia, and I'm going to hospice this afternoon. All my things, my house. ... Well, none of this matters to you, Agnes. Agnes with the name that will last. I can say this, though. Quit the things you need to. And the things you can't, well ... you might as well enjoy them right up until the end." He unrolled the slip of paper and breathed out as he stared at the words. "Will you please tell Martha I sent her my regards?"

Agnes nodded. She didn't trust herself to speak.

"Thank you, my dear." The man stood, and she could see now how fragile he was beneath that cotton shirt. Why did it matter? Yet, she was surprised to find that it did. "You have a lovely day. It's just starting, don't you know?"

The waitress watched him shuffle out, and she didn't know if she felt like laughing or crying. Maybe a little of both.

WE MOVE AS DUST

Mike Bernicchi

There were missions at dusk, sometimes
neon moon pulsing the sky,
so I pretend it's a room,
and we're unsupervised children
shuffling our feet on the carpet—
lightning carried like a word,
sleep comes with the rain;
we move as dust.

We line up detainees in a procession,
upright and yellowed like elegant candles, though
some are gold—precious cargo—and we
are mailmen essentially
with most-wanted cards
woven in the decks
of frigates we could fly
to Babylon, sometimes Basra—
they somehow knew the difference,
but Sulamaniyah does
look alotlike Denver in the   spring

and i say *shweya*
when youssif offers me tea
and we wonder
how baghdad stays green in the summer
when beckham is spilledlikesalt
for translating words
icould never understand
and i never slept again
not in nasiriyah not
in basra when the brits
dropped shells
like candy on thekids
and im six watching pinatas
in a palm tree pattern on the sand
vehicles are acrobats
and i rock back and forth
in unison
with the road   hushed
and the turret creaks like it moans
for a rest   but it wont
and i just got here and it's
still   yesterday

THE ELEPHANT IN THE BATHTUB

J. Lewis Fleming

CHARACTERS:

- RUFUS HIGHWATER: aging, eccentric former gold miner
- EDWINA HIGHWATER: young, gorgeous second wife of Rufus
- JERROD RUBY: handsome, desperate young man in search of employment

The play takes place in a ramshackle basement room of the Hotel Barbary.

At RISE:
(A basement room of the Hotel Barbary. It is not long after the famous gold rush of 1849. The men who struck it rich, like RUFUS HIGHWATER, have been living the high life, and the men who didn't—men like JERROD RUBY—have been scrabbling in the dirt just to get by. The time of day is impossible to tell, owing to the fact that this room has no windows. Rufus is propped on an old wooden chair left center stage, facing down right center. The chair is nestled up to a battered, old wooden table. Another chair waits on the opposite side of the table. Rufus scratches furiously at a piece of paper with the small nub of a pencil. EDWINA HIGHWATER sits just down left of Rufus, facing roughly the same direction. She is in an elegant high-backed chair with a pad of paper balanced on her crossed legs. Edwina holds a ridiculous feather quill pen in her hand, poised above the paper and ready to write. She gazes wistfully out at the audience. A clawfoot tub lingers up right center.)

(For several long moments, Rufus is writing, and Edwina is staring.)

RUFUS: *(Voice gruff, even when not angry, he slams down pencil stub, growling in frustration.)* Argh!

EDWINA: *(Still staring into the audience, wistful, but hopeful.)* What is it, Roo?

RUFUS: *(Rubbing his temples and staring down at the paper in front of him.)* It's this damn list, Ed. *(Pausing, he turns to look at Edwina, who continues staring into the audience.)* You sure about all this? Look at the list of no-account hooligans who've been through here already.

EDWINA: Rufus, darling, we've talked this thing through from beginning to end. I offered up several other ideas, each of which you poo-pooed, and this was the only option left. And you agreed. Remember?

RUFUS: *(Begins to grumble but is cut short.)* Err ...

EDWINA: And just because we haven't found the right man yet. ... Well, did you give up the first time a gold prospect came up empty? Or the second? Or the third?

RUFUS: Well, 'course not, but ...

EDWINA: Do you love me?

RUFUS: Aw, Ed.

EDWINA: Do you?

RUFUS: *(Softly but intensely.)* Hellfire, Ed, 'course I do.

EDWINA: *(Looks at Rufus, smiling adoringly.)* Okay, then. *(She points with a gentle sort of reproach at the paper in front of Rufus.)*

RUFUS: *(Turns back to the table. Picking up the nub of a pencil, he begins chewing the end while studying the paper in front of him.)* Fine, fine. You're right. Next one'll be here any minute now. *(Reading from sheet in front of him.)* Jerrod Ruby.

EDWINA: What's that?

RUFUS: The next fella. Name of Jerrod Ruby.

EDWINA: I like that name. Very ... *(Pause.)* Pleasant.

RUFUS: *(Grunts softly and shrugs his shoulders.)* Humph. *(There is a knock at the door offstage right.)* Speak of the devil. *(Hollering.)* GET IN HERE!

JERROD: *(Entering timidly, hat in hand, playing nervously with the wide brim.)* Uh ... hello. I'm ... uh ... here about the ... uh ... job, advertisement, posting, thing. *(Snaps his mouth shut, as though the words are coming out against his will.)*

RUFUS: *(Gruff, but not unkind.)* Sit, my boy. No need to be nervous. *(Glances quickly at Edwina, who smiles briefly in response.)* You must be Jerrod Ruby.

JERROD: *(Reaches to doff his hat, not realizing it is already in his hand, and smacks himself in the mouth with the wide brim.)* Uh ... yes ... yes, sir, I am he ... sir.

RUFUS: *(Gesturing toward the empty chair.)* Have a seat, my boy.

JERROD: *(Glances nervously toward the door where he entered, then at the seat, then at Rufus' extended hand, then at the door, then at Edwina, then at the seat. Finally seems to muster a small amount of nerve and moves forward, only to see the bathtub for the first time and to stop in his tracks. He gathers himself and rushes to the chair, knocking it to the floor. Attempting to right the chair, he falls over it, landing near Edwina's feet. He looks up into her face, seeing an angelic smile, and a preternatural calm suddenly comes over him. He rights himself, then the chair, all while gazing at Edwina.)* Yes, sir. Thank you, sir. *(He begins to sit.)*

RUFUS: Actually, you best get in the tub first.

JERROD: Uh ... the tub ... sir?

RUFUS: *(Pointing.)* The tub.

EDWINA: We have to see if you fit, dear.

JERROD: Fit?

EDWINA: In the tub. That's right.

JERROD: *(Moving slowly toward the tub.)* You ... need to see if I ... fit ... in the tub?

EDWINA: *(Nodding and smiling.)* That's right.

JERROD: *(Still moving slowly toward tub. Looking first at Edwina, then at Rufus, then at the tub, finally at Rufus again.)* Is this? Is this part of the job or ...

RUFUS: Yep. Pretty damn important part, truth be told.

JERROD: *(Putting first one foot and then the other in the tub, he slowly lowers himself to a sitting position, stopping and starting all the while as though he's never been in a bathtub before.)* Like this?

EDWINA: *(Rises and glides over to the tub. She walks around until she is behind Jerrod. She puts her hands gently on his shoulders and pushes down.)* Actually, dear, if you could lie all the way down. That's right, very good. *(Speaking now to Rufus.)* Perfect, right, my love?

RUFUS: Good enough, I suppose. Okay, boy, you can come sit in this here chair now.

JERROD: *(Nodding, rising from the tub and slinking over to the chair. He sits. Edwina returns to her chair at the same time.)* I don't ... think I really understand all this. The ad said something about a life-changing experience and ... well ... I guess I never imagined that it would involve a bathtub.

(Edwina and Rufus both laugh. His is somewhat rueful and loud. Hers is equally loud but full of genuine mirth.)

JERROD: Did ... did I say something funny? I'm afraid I feel more than a bit off the rails. Like I've wandered into someone else's dream.

EDWINA: *(Smiling, her hands clasped together.)* Oh, he's just precious. *(Looking at Rufus.)* Can we keep him, my love?

RUFUS: *(Scratching his chin, thinking, and eyeballing the young man, but speaking to himself as though ticking off a list.)* Well dressed. Well spoken. Bit nervous. Handsome enough, I s'pose. Fits in the tub. *(Addressing Jerrod.)* You ain't got any weird marks or deformities, do ya?

JERROD: *(More nervous now than ever.)* Weird ... deformities? *(Trying to sound offended but failing and sounding frightened instead.)* What ... what do you mean?

RUFUS: You know, like a tail or six toes on your left foot? Somethin' like that?

JERROD: *(Glancing quickly at Edwina, then back to Rufus.)* What? I ... no. Most assuredly not.

RUFUS: Well, that's a relief. We had this one guy in here, you would not believe. *(Gesturing suggestively with his hands.)* His johnson was so ...

EDWINA: *(Calmly, patiently interrupting.)* Now, now, my love. The young man doesn't need to hear that story.

RUFUS: *(Examining Jerrod.)* I suppose not.

JERROD: *(After a long moment of silence, nervously begins speaking.)* This is a job interview, isn't it?

RUFUS: *(Nodding matter-of-factly.)* 'Course.

JERROD: Could you tell me a bit more about the job ... or, really, anything? I don't believe you've given me a single detail of the work. And this thing with the clawfoot ...

RUFUS: Well, this here's a sensitive subject, Jerrod. You've passed the eyeball test, you've passed the manners test, you seem like a bright fella, and, most important, you've passed the tub test. You got the right kind of, what's the word, Ed?

EDWINA: *(Smiling at Jerrod, speaking in perfect French and gesticulating gracefully.)* Je ne sais quoi.

RUFUS: *(Smiling at Edwina.)* Yeah. That's the one. *(Turning back to Jerrod and whispering.)* I love when she talks French. *(Clearing his throat and speaking again in a normal tone.)* So ... I guess we can move on. To put it in simple terms: you've passed the test, Jerrod, and we're prepared to offer you the job. *(Looking at Edwina.)* That about right, dear?

EDWINA: *(Nodding happily and gazing hungrily at Jerrod.)* Oh, yes. He's certainly passed. Passed with excellent marks. Very handsome.

RUFUS: All right, son. Here's how it is: me and the wife ... *(Gesturing and smiling at Edwina.)* Well, we been trying for years, you see, but we can't exactly ... you know ... we haven't been able to ...

EDWINA: *(Blurting, but with a quiet dignity.)* I want a baby.

RUFUS: Yeah, but here's the thing. It hasn't happened yet, and Lord knows we've been trying our hardest.

EDWINA: Yes. Trying and trying and trying.

RUFUS: Right. So that's where you come in, son.

EDWINA: So to speak.

JERROD: *(Looking at Edwina in complete confusion. Turning toward Rufus with dawning understanding.)* You ... want ... me to ... *(Looking at Edwina again.)*

EDWINA: *(Smiling and nodding.)* Mmmm.

JERROD: Ah ... *(Searching for just the right word.)* ... Help?

RUFUS: *(Smiling, impressed.)* Damn, boy, that was well said. You got you some book learning, I bet.

JERROD: *(Looking stunned.)* Yes, sir. Some. I ...

EDWINA: It's very simple, Jerrod. You lay with me and help me get the baby boy I want, the heir for our family that my husband ... that *we* could not get ourselves.

JERROD: *(Looking and sounding dismayed, but attempting to remain polite and understanding at all costs.)* That's the job?

RUFUS: That's the job.

EDWINA: That's the job.

JERROD: *(Sounding a little sarcastic and showing cracks in his polite façade. Sounding more and more frantic, but remaining at a conversational tone. Staring down at his fidgeting hands.)* That's it. Just that little task. Lay with your wife. That's the job. That's it. That's the job. Just that easy. Lay with another man's wife. Give her a baby. That's it. That's all.

RUFUS: Well, there's a bit more to it. This being such a sensitive thing, and times being what they are ...

JERROD: *(Looking at Rufus, regaining some of his calm demeanor.)* You need me to be quiet about it.

EDWINA: *(Softly, quietly.)* Silent. Like the grave.

JERROD: Like the grave?

RUFUS & EDWINA: Like the grave.

(The whole company is silent, lost in their own thoughts. Jerrod is looking around furtively, as though planning his escape.)

RUFUS: Before we continue, would you like to discuss your renumeration?

JERROD: *(Looking up at Rufus in confusion.)* My what? *(Pauses, thinking.)* You mean remuneration?

EDWINA: That's what he means, dear.

RUFUS: You know, payment. Your fee? Don't you want to know what it'll be?

JERROD: *(Nodding distractedly.)* I ... I suppose. Though I'm not sure I feel completely comfortable with this.

RUFUS: Which part?

JERROD: Which ... part?

RUFUS: The laying with my wife part?

JERROD: Yes, sir. I mean, we're sitting here, very politely discussing my having intimate, carnal, and sinful affairs with your wife.

RUFUS: What's the matter? You don't want to?

JERROD: Well ... I ...

RUFUS: *(An edge coming into his voice.)* Something wrong with my wife, boy?

JERROD: God ... no ... she's ... she's stunning.

RUFUS: *(Edwina and Rufus looking pointedly at Jerrod's crotch.)* Something wrong with you?

JERROD: Absolutely not. It's just, this is a sin, sir. And one in which you seem to be gladly taking part. If this were to get out ... the stigma ... your wife. This is your wife, sir.

RUFUS: *(Growling.)* Damn right, boy. *My* wife. Mine. And this won't get out 'cause we ain't gonna let it.

JERROD: No, no, of course. ... It's just ... it's just a bit overwhelming.

EDWINA: *(Gliding over to Jerrod and placing her hands once again on his shoulders.)* It is a difficult thing, Jerrod, but please understand that Rufus and I have been discussing this possibility for years. We are both of one mind about it. We accept that it is ... unusual and are prepared to do anything to make sure that this union produces a son without rumor or suspicion. All parties will remain unblemished in the eyes of the citizenry of San Francisco and beyond.

JERROD: And if the child turns out to be a girl?

EDWINA: Well, that won't be any of your concern. Rufus and I would merely move on.

JERROD: You'd find someone else, then?

EDWINA: Correct.

JERROD: I ... I need some time to think about this.

RUFUS: 'Fraid not. Need you to decide now.

JERROD: *(Searching desperately for the right words, trying to buy himself time to think.)* All right, so if I say no, what happens?

(Rufus says nothing, but points toward the exit door offstage right.)

EDWINA: And we would need your word that you would say nothing of this to anyone.

RUFUS: *(Calm, but with a menacing undertone.)* 'Cause if you did ... well, things'd get *real* uncomfortable for you. And the wife and I'd just deny it, 'cause who are you anyway? Nobody. And nobody'd believe you.

JERROD: *(Nodding.)* Of course, of course. And if I say yes? When does this happen?

RUFUS: *(Pointing over his shoulder to offstage left.)* Right now. Got everything set behind that door, there.

JERROD: *(To himself, sarcastically.)* Right, right. Okay. Wonderful. Right now. Fantastic. That's ... *(Looking up at Rufus and seeing the anger dawning in the man's eyes.)* So, payment, I guess? Although, frankly, at this point, I can't honestly say that I'm really considering this ...

EDWINA: Jerrod, we really need your help ... want your help. We've had a dozen young men in here, and you are the only one who has lived up to our standards. You've exceeded them in a way that we could have only prayed for ... we have prayed for. You *are* the answer to our prayers, and here you are. We need you. *(Pause.)* I need you. *(Edwina returns to her chair.)*

JERROD: *(Sounding gentlemanly.)* In that case, ma'am, I must at least listen to your offer. *(Turning back to Rufus.)* What is your offer, sir?

RUFUS: *(With a wicked smile.)* A fortune in gold.

JERROD: *(Swallowing hard, trying to contain his surprise and excitement. This could be the break he was looking for, after all.)* A fortune ... in ... gold?

RUFUS: Yep.

JERROD: Just how much gold are we talking about?

RUFUS: *(Handing Jerrod the pencil nub and a piece of paper.)* You tell me.

JERROD: *(Taking the pencil in a shaking hand, thinking for a moment, and then, writing in a mad dash.)* Here. *(He pushes the pencil and paper back to Rufus.)*

RUFUS: *(Reading the paper and then extending his right hand.)* Deal.

JERROD: *(Leaping to his feet.)* What?!

RUFUS: Deal.

JERROD: You would actually pay me that amount to lay with your wife.

EDWINA: *(Leaning forward to read the paper.)* Oh yes, dear, that sum and more.

RUFUS: *(Still holding out his right hand.)* Deal?

JERROD: *(Looking unbelievingly at Rufus and Edwina and seeing nothing but sincerity, Jerrod pauses then speaks wistfully.)* I ... I ... I don't see how I can refuse that kind of money. *(Seizing Rufus' hand in his own, pumping it furiously, a dam breaks and his emotions flood out.)* Oh, God, you have no idea what this will do for us.

EDWINA: *(Sounding a little concerned.)* Us, dear?

JERROD: *(Turning to Edwina, full of enthusiasm.)* My niece and twin nephews, my mother. They've been living with me for about a year now. I'm the only family they have left. I'm ashamed to say we've been nearly starving because I haven't had steady work in all that time, and the twins have taken ill. Frankly, I had just about given up hope, when I saw your advertisement. I figured it was a sham, too good to be true, you understand, but I've been so desperate I decided to answer it anyway. *(Is overcome, sits down, and falls silent. After a long pause, breathing deeply, and continuing much more slowly.)* My God, I cannot wait to see the looks on their faces when I show them such a fortune. We're ... we're saved. *(Turning to Rufus.)* I will do it, sir. I will do it.

RUFUS: *(Looking to Edwina, who nods slowly, knowingly, in return.)* Well, now, me and the wife are surely glad to hear that. Yes, indeed, that gladdens the heart.

(All three fall silent, filled with their own thoughts. They are each happy in their own way.)

JERROD: *(Has stopped weeping and dabs at his eyes with a handkerchief.)* Just out of curiosity, why did you need me to sit in the tub?

RUFUS: Well, we can't have you makin' a mess all over the floor down here.

JERROD: Mess?

RUFUS: Sure. Bound to be messy. These things usually are.

JERROD: *(Looking more uncomfortable than he has the entire time on stage.)* Uh ... pardon me, sir, but my understanding was that ... uh ... your wife and I ... whose name I just realized I never got ... that ... we were to ... you know ... lay together in that room back there. *(Points. Then looks from Rufus to Edwina.)*

RUFUS: Edwina.

JERROD: Um ... sorry?

RUFUS: *(Motioning toward Edwina.)* Edwina. My wife. I call her Ed, but only *I* call her Ed. Got that?

JERROD: *(Nodding, still confused.)* Yes, sir, but ... *(Clearing his throat and pointing at the bathtub.)* Do you intend us to lay together in the clawfoot, sir?

EDWINA: *(Shocked in a humorous way.)* Dear me, no. That would truly be the devil on my back! The bathtub is for after.

(Jerrod still looks confused.)

EDWINA: For the suicide, dear.

JERROD: Su ... did ... uh ... did you say 'suicide'?

EDWINA: *(Very pleasantly, as though this conversation were perfectly normal.)* Well, of course. We can't very well have you leaving here alive and sharing our secret with your friends or your family. *(Pauses.)* Or your pastor. *(Pauses, sizing Jerrod up.)* Or your bartender.

JERROD: *(Looking wildly at Rufus.)* You ...? You expect me to ...? You actually think I'd ...?

EDWINA: Of course, dear. Why do you think we're prepared to reward you so handsomely for your efforts? Pity? Kindness? Not hardly. We are asking you to perform a difficult task, and we are prepared to pay your survivors very handsomely for that service. No offense intended, but can you imagine *me* paying to lay with someone like yourself?

RUFUS: *(Snorting in laughter, but not unkindly, pointing at Edwina.)* My wife ... *(Pointing to Jerrod.)* Payin' you ... *(Pointing offstage.)* For that? *(Continues to laugh as Edwina joins in with a soft, friendly titter of her own.)*

JERROD: *(Slowly looking back and forth from Edwina to Rufus as their laughter fades to gentle smiles. He is clearly parsing out if this is some kind of demented joke and seeing in their faces that it is not. He is silent for a time, then finds his resolve.)* Can ... can I see that number ... one more time?

(Rufus picks up the slip of paper on which Jerrod has written his fee. He glances at it briefly and hands it to Jerrod. Jerrod takes the paper in his hand, staring at it for a long moment.)

(CURTAIN)

After Abandon

Michael Cooper

give up the star sky for the comfort
of vaulted ceiling fan, spin
the sweet saw sound and vagrant—
your knee invades my spine dressed
in rag picker's flannel
                        Coverstealer. One
of our arms always   useless   Skeleton
of your body next to mine—twin
picket fences that lay their guard down
slowly—the wheat
                    climbs over, gossips;
the night star smiles open where

our brows meet—and you, dreaming,
each of us a pulse, a thumb
                        print in a
thousand untranslatable Polaroids—
taken
        by this dark room.

An American Seeker

Kevin Catalano

Heidi returned from her job at the Watchung Bank and Loan that evening, glad to find that Paul had already left for work. For the first time in their four-year relationship, Heidi began snooping through Paul's things. The cargo shorts Paul had worn while tending bar were balled up on the carpet next to his side of the bed. They were dank with alcohol and sweat. She turned the pockets inside-out and wads of cash fell to the floor, along with receipts and business cards. Heidi sat cross-legged and sifted through the evidence, heart racing with expectation. The business cards were not at all interesting (mainly because they belonged to men). However, the receipts had suspicious things written on them. Many had phone numbers and email addresses, though no names; one had drawings of stick figures with stick dicks going into stick vaginas; another, the one that really got Heidi's attention, had the words *American Psycho* written in a female's bubbly script with a heart next to it. This receipt she held on to.

Since last night, Heidi was disturbed that Paul had managed to surprise her with the marriage proposal. They were at the same semi-authentic Italian restaurant they'd always gone to Sunday nights, and three different waitresses delivered three different, ever-since-the-day-I-met-you lines, concluding with big Paul, wincing on a knee, displaying a ring.

Heidi thought she knew him well enough to tell when he was keeping something from her. In fact, he no longer attempted to surprise her with Christmas or birthday gifts. Now, he simply asked what she wanted, because she'd find the receipt for the gift, or the gift itself stupidly hidden in places he never frequented, which were the exact places she always did: the top of the coat closet where the iron was kept, under the kitchen sink with the glass cleaner and dishwasher detergent—inside the washing machine, for Christ's sake. Heidi didn't like the version of herself that knew more about Paul than Paul did. She hated being *that* kind of woman, the type depicted in sitcoms and women's magazines—the ones who nag their dopey husbands. But if dopey Paul was capable of secretly planning such an elaborate proposal, he could be capable of any other imaginable sneakiness.

She knew the night would conclude with her sitting at the kitchen table, well into her third glass of pinot noir, Paul's laptop open, looking through his emails. She logged onto his account, typing in the same password he used for everything: *Paul123*.

Two thousand unread emails. She instinctively wanted to organize his messages, deleting the obvious junk emails, creating folders for the others. But she was on a mission, searching for messages from girls. Maybe *American Psycho* was a codeword he used when emailing some lonely housewife for a late-night hook-up. She did a quick Google search and discovered *American Psycho* was a novel, which only intrigued her more, since Paul wasn't a reader. She then typed the phrase into the email's search, but came up with nothing. She scrolled through pages and pages of messages, clicking on the ones from females whose names were unfamiliar. A few got her attention. One from last year read: "Hope to see you this weekend," to which he had replied, "Right on"—a phrase he unfortunately overused. Mostly, these messages were harmless, though she wouldn't allow herself to quit until she had exhausted her search. She kept telling herself *one more page*. And then, it was one o'clock in the morning.

She felt disgusting. Her legs were cramped from sitting in the chair at the kitchen table. The entire apartment was dark, except for the blue light of the laptop screen. She groaned and got up to pee, avoiding herself in the bathroom mirror. The same impulse that compelled her to snoop, however, forced her to examine her reflection. Closely. She forced a smile, then let it limp, and studied the lines left behind. So close the mirror fogged, she held her breath, and noted her freckles turning to the splotches her mother now had on her face and hands. Heidi stared hard at herself, a ruthless showdown. She shut out the lights, darkness crawling her skin.

She muttered, "Fuck you, you old, worthless bitch."

Here was the plan: when Paul woke up tomorrow, Heidi would be reading *American Psycho* on the couch, so that when he came out of the bedroom, she and the book would be the first thing he saw. Over the top of the pages she'd carefully watch for his expression, that which would give him away. Once trapped, she'd pounce—interrogating him until he confessed his infidelity. She would have to prepare for what he might reveal: an affair that had gone on for years, perhaps with not only one woman, but countless female customers—hundreds maybe. Perhaps he never worked at the bar; maybe that was a cover for cheating, and he was even savvier than she recently thought. She had to be ready for anything.

There was nothing on TV that night—nothing else to do other than read the book. She hadn't planned on reading it; the book was a prop. She wouldn't admit this to most people, but her reading material of choice was vampire and sorcery and King Arthur books. They didn't write these novels fast enough. She knew very well that these were what thirteen-year-old girls read—that they were considered lowbrow and so forth. But they were good, and when she was home alone at night, she wasn't looking to challenge her intellect or broaden her horizons. She was just looking for a good read, and maybe if these literary authors got off their high horses and wrote something interesting for a change, she'd give them a try.

Heidi put on her soft, froggy pajamas, poured herself some wine, got under a blanket on the couch, and opened this novel with the horrible name. At first, she didn't get it. There was this egotistical guy who apparently loved face- and hair-product, who loved to exercise and listen to 80s music, and who hung out with Wall Street friends who were shallow and racist and talked about nothing other than getting reservations at fancy restaurants. Where was the psycho stuff? Heidi kept looking at the book cover to make sure she had the right one. This is so stupid, she thought, but found it rather easy to read—not a lot of big words or fancy writing. She was over a hundred pages in when the guy narrating the book, Patrick, sliced open a homeless man's eyeball, and it ran down his face like an egg yolk. Then Patrick cut open the man's nose, and the most awful part was that he didn't kill the man; he just left him in agony on the street, with his eye cut out and his nose flayed.

"Jesus," Heidi said to the book, heart throbbing in her ears. What surprised Heidi, scared her a little, was that she began to read faster, seeking out the next violent scene.

The violence to come was unimaginable horror, and she read voraciously. This Patrick would lure various women into his extravagant Manhattan apartment, and do unspeakable things to them with mace, a nail gun, a rusty coat hanger, a power drill, and oh, Lord, what he did to one with a rat. Reading these scenes—described so carefully, in such gruesome detail—made Heidi afraid of herself. The author's trick, if it was one, was that what preceded the violence were detailed, pornographic sex scenes, so that Heidi constantly found her hand between her legs. Then, out would come the nail gun! She was convinced she was diseased in the head, the furious way she was devouring the pages, reading (hoping?) for how the author would top the previous scene's gruesomeness.

The handle of the front door jiggled. Heidi froze. It was three a.m. Thank God it was only Paul. She remembered the book, the plan—this could all backfire if he found her on the couch waiting up for him.

Paul opened the door, and Heidi hid the book under the blanket. He looked at her, confused, and then he smiled. "Hey, baby. What are you doing up?"

"Nothing," was all she managed. She noticed that the TV was off, the apartment was dark, and there was no type of reading material in sight. She must have looked creepy.

"Nothing?" he stumbled toward her, a little tipsy. He sat down next to her, unloading wads of cash onto the coffee table. "What do you mean, nothing? What were you doing?"

It was late. She was suddenly tired and irritated that she was in this position. "Just nothing, Paul," she snapped. "Leave me alone."

His big, flushed face retained the smile, and now the sweet scent of liquor wafted from his mouth. "You've been acting really weird lately. Ever since I proposed to you."

Heidi bunched up the blanket to conceal the book and waddled to the bedroom. She was aware, and ashamed of her behavior, but couldn't help it.

Paul followed her into the room. "If you don't want to get married," he said, "we don't have to. We'll just go back to how it was before."

She climbed into bed, still holding the balled-up blanket. "How it was before," she repeated absently. The hard spine of the novel had found its way between her legs. She shifted her butt to escape it, but it only pressed into her, prickling her thighs with goosebumps.

Then Paul said, "What are you hiding?"

She shook her head.

"Under the blanket. I'm not an idiot."

The book rubbed at her clitoris. She bit her lip, squinted her eyes.

Paul stood still watching her for a moment. "You're losing it," he said, and left the room.

Heidi slithered under the covers and squeezed her eyes shut. The violent images from the novel were waiting for her. One scene in particular described Patrick skinning a woman alive. Heidi felt that about herself, that someone was yanking her skin off her flesh in one, long peel, revealing the purple meat underneath.

Paul had slept on the couch that night, which he often did; this time, though, he was sending her a message. So as not to wake him, she sneaked out the bedroom and through the kitchen glowing with new sun. She went into the bathroom and sat on the toilet. Her head buzzed, hung over from the late night and her gruesome dreams.

She turned on the shower and studied herself in the mirror. There, on the split of her nose, a cold sore was blossoming. It was in its pre-pus stage, bubbling the skin. Of course she would get one—it was her punishment for her behavior. She always understood her cold sores to be what kept her vanity in check. This morning, however, she surprised herself. She pulled the tip of her nose up oink-style and studied the viral skin— the pinks and reds, the tumor-like texture that deformed her. Where before she would want to hide under a rock for the week, today she couldn't wait for the ooze, the gold-flaked crust of dried pus. Her own distinct, localized horror show.

Instead of going to work, she drove to the mall. She weaved in and out of the elderly mall-walkers and teenagers, and stopped at a mannequin in the window of one of those boutiques that sells slutty, urban-youth apparel. The mannequin sported a fabulous black dress with a low V-neck top and a dangerously short skirt. She wore knee-high black fuck-me boots, and to top it off, a raven-black, femme fatale wig. She'd walked by this display countless times in the past few weeks, always intrigued, not sure why.

"Patricia," Heidi said, fogging the glass.

She charged into the store and ordered the sixteen-year-old texting on her phone to retrieve the dress and boots. The girl was exasperated and moved too slowly, so Heidi stepped into the showcase window and stripped the mannequin. She shimmied out of her clothes, putting on a show for the group of high-school guys who stopped to gawk. She performed a catwalk twirl before pulling on the black dress, then stepped into the boots, and zipped them up her calf with slow seduction. After positioning the wig on her head, she cocked her hip and blew a kiss at the guys—who hooted and took pictures of her on their phones—and she turned and marched out of the window.

"Hey, you can't do that," the teenager called.

"It's already done."

As she strutted through the mall toward the exit, Heidi felt that the blood pumping through her had electrified, sending continuous spasms up and down her legs. She got into her car, deciding right at that moment that she—or rather, Patricia—was going to pay Paul a visit at the bar.

As she drove, she thought of the times—at least twice a year—when she would get so fed up with Paul's messiness and overall lack of drive that she'd blow up at him and demand that he make an attempt to change. For a solid week, he'd clean up his hairs from the bathroom sink, put his dishes away, and make the bed. Once he even typed up a résumé, but the only jobs it listed were a Staples and the same bar he'd been tending ever since they met, which was at the bank. At that time, she was a lowly teller, and every couple weeks, he'd deposit startling wads of cash. There was plenty of time to chat as she counted the filthy bills—organizing them into sequential piles—that amounted to six-to-eight hundred dollars. She would think about his mysterious profession at night in bed: a drug dealer, a ruthless bookie, a pool-playing hustler. In each scenario, she would be his fabulous accountant. This was his allure, and so she had allowed him to take her out to dinner where she couldn't wait to ask what he did for a living. Her disappointment was profound when he told her he tended bar. But as the meal progressed, she had found herself charmed by his humor and affability. Even if he wasn't New Jersey's leading supplier of marijuana, there was still something enigmatic about Paul that kept her interested. Perhaps, she now thought, it was his inability to change—that he remained the same old Paul despite his context. Or maybe the fact was that nobody was capable of change, and therefore, Paul was just like everybody else.

Heidi squealed into the parking lot of the bar. She looked at herself in the rearview and adjusted the black wig. Her cold sore was oozing, an orange, candy-like bubble. As Heidi stepped out of the car, she wondered whether she was evidence that people change. She charged toward the entrance with supermodel confidence—wagging her ass and swinging her arms, heels clapping the asphalt like nail-gun fire. This was not change, she thought. This was finding herself.

Heidi flung open the door and swaggered inside. She wanted to see if Paul was into the dangerous types, because he might have to marry one.

Sewing

Noel King

I have a need to cover a great oak tree with one
big white sheet, dream of threading together
a house-full pulled from under a family
who stare at me, consider me mad; brutal even.

At eight, I fell from its branches, don't know what
happened then, just remember being bedridden.
At ten, I crouched in lightning, not knowing a tree
was the last place to shelter.

An oak swish in winter soothed me at earlier times
of life. Now its tongues tease me, coming as it has before
baby, child, teenager, husband, widower. Naked
in a nightmare, I am barely balanced on my garden wall,

wave my arms to keep balance and the sheet in my hands
from flapping, despair on how to get my sheet over the tree.
I no longer object to house plans for its field, won't mind
the sound of a chainsaw; will a dream to sit on

its wide stump as branches lay dying in the grass, and I
won't count the circles, knowing it has lived long enough.

Cause Célèbre

Andrei Guruianu

It seems just yesterday we were out on the parapets
demanding an audience with congress.
Took turns admiring the parade of self-inflicted wounds.

Now empty shells make lonely topics of conversation
and so do the well-oiled pistols collecting dust behind glass.
We've run out of things to rally against.

About dinnertime, every spoon of the recent past tastes insipid.
Old women's breasts flop onto the table;
men claim elbow room and pull at their graying beards—

their bandoliers limp on a hook on a door
along with the wool coat and rabbit fur hat.
A crushed fire burning in every living room ashtray.

Inheritance

Stephanie Liden

A cluster of meadowlarks covers the snowy highway in front of my father's 1962 Ford Falcon. The birds flee the road just as I pass them by. I watch as the flock expands apart, and in the rearview, the larks regroup to pick at a frozen raccoon carcass. After I pass a small patch of pine trees, the wind forces the car to the center of the road, and I quickly correct. I wonder why these meadowlarks stick around, why they endure like they do. I shift on the white leather seat. I am in my father's spot—the driver's seat—seeing our rural prairie homeland from his point of view. My friend, Sasha, is by my side. We handed in our two-weeks' notice at the gas station together. Today was our last day. Before we left, she stole our favorite postcard of a Malibu sunset, a lighter, and a pack of cigarettes. She put the card on the passenger visor, a glossy reminder of where we will go—palm trees and pink skies. I gassed up the Falcon, and here we are, on the way to pick up my father from treatment—one last thing before we leave.

"I love this car," Sasha says, twisting the radio's ivory knob, turning up the volume.

I thumb the smooth leather steering wheel cover and see my dad, a dirty rag in his back pocket, leaning over the open hood, up to his elbows in engine. The smell of turtle wax and glycerin. I twist the ivory knob back down.

"I'm warning you," I say. "My father's crazy."

She blows an egg-shaped pink bubble, and it pops. "I have a crazy uncle. He lives in the desert, in a hut made from glass soda bottles."

"Bullshit."

"It's true. The bottles absorb heat in the day and keep him warm all night." Sasha pulls a pack of Marlboro Reds from her purse and peels the cellophane.

"My dad would kill me if he knew we were smoking in here."

She lights it with a gas-station Bic.

"He's worked on this car ever since I can remember," I say.

"Fuck him," she says.

For a quick moment, I feel like I should defend him, but it passes. Sasha knows my father hasn't been well for a while, but that's it. I want to tell her the truth. That I remember the first moment I noticed something wasn't right. I came into my room to find my father installing locks on the windows. His eyes wild, he said, "We need to take every precaution, kiddo." I laughed it off at the time. The last time I saw my father, I came home from work to the red and blue cop lights flashing against the Falcon's frosted windows. I could see the lights from the highway.

The officer said my father had been drinking when he threatened my grandmother with a steak knife, but we all knew it was more than booze. When he was admitted to treatment, my grandmother went to a nursing home, and I stayed alone on the farm. The farm where my father and I grew up, a rambler with a wraparound porch, surrounded by pines. One Quonset, one barn. My grandfather made my father a tire swing, and it hangs by the porch to this day, the ground beneath it worn away from years of our dragging feet. But the place never really felt like home. The stoic silence filled every room, and the walls are white and empty. None of my memories of that place are in color.

A gust of cold winter wind seeps into the car through the cracked window, and I tuck loose strands of hair behind my ear. I crank the handle on the door, and the window squeaks closed.

"Your hair is pretty. You should let it down," Sasha says, tugging softly at my braid. Her touch is gentle, affectionate.

A truck passes us slowly. The woman in the passenger seat looks at me for a moment, and then speaks to the man driving. The look on her face is subtle, but I have seen it before. Once when my grandmother and her friends gossiped over coffee. The sheriff's wife left him for another woman, and the whole town knew.

"Oughta be ashamed," my grandmother said.

I tense, and Sasha stops touching my hair. I want to tell her not to quit, but I don't. I am ashamed of that.

"Beautiful Arapaho hair," Sasha says. The only physical part of me that comes from my mother's Native American background. My father and grandmother insisted I never cut my hair.

"Keep it long, or they'll think you're a boy," my grandmother said.

"Keep it long; you look like your mother," my father said.

The winter wind forces the car to shake even more as we pass miles of barren fields, empty brown and white space as far as the eye can see. I turn up the heat, and the windows begin to cloud. There's an abandoned house in a clump of trees ahead. A small, single-story farmhouse, the white paint chipped away. The roof sags under the weight of snow. In the yard, there is a sign with faded letters that spell: "Velkommen." Relics of another time, from uprooted Norwegian farmers.

"What a shithole," Sasha says as we pass.

"Yeah." It needs new shingles and some paint, for sure. As we drive by, I wonder if this place was ever a home.

I pull the Falcon into the hospital parking lot and find a place close to the sliding-door entrance. I watch Sasha apply dark, black eyeliner in the rearview mirror.

"I can tell you're a little nervous," she says. "Let me help you."

She slides close to me. She smells like cigarettes and bubblegum. She tells me to close my eyes, and I do. I think for a moment how my father hates when I wear makeup. He would tell me that naturally beautiful women don't need it and that my mother never did. But I don't look like her, and I don't care what he thinks anymore. I feel Sasha's soft fingertips on my cheek and then the sharp end of the pencil against my closed lid.

"There," she says. "You look good."

"War paint," I joke.

We walk through the sliding doors, and my father is waiting by the nurses station, his army-green duffel in hand. I ask Sasha to stay by the door. My father smiles when he sees me, like he hasn't seen a familiar face in a while, like a dog being picked up from the vet. He wears navy blue sweats, a dark gray sweatshirt, and heavy work boots. He still has a thick gray and brown beard, but a new thinning crew cut. He fidgets with a plastic bracelet that has his name and contact information for the hospital.

"Thanks for picking me up," he says, and we shake hands for what feels like a long time. His skin is soft, and he smells sanitized. I search his face for signs that he might lash out, cry, yell, any indication of emotion, but there is nothing. He looks away, fidgets with his bracelet.

"Want me to get the nurse to cut that off for you?"

"Naw, I'll keep it on for a little while." He notices Sasha standing by the sliding door. She smiles, but her arms are crossed, and she leans on one hip. "I thought we would have some time alone on the drive, kiddo." He looks at his shoes.

"We need to get going," I say. "Getting dark." When we get to the door, I introduce him to Sasha, and they exchange quick hellos. She looks him up and down, her eyes like a spotlight. He leads the way out of the hospital entrance. The name "Miller" is screenprinted across his duffel, but the letters are so faded now that you can barely make them out.

When we get to the car, he pats the trunk gently and runs his fingers along the subtle grooves. "There she is," he says. "I'm driving."

"You can't drive," I say and help my father pack his duffel into the trunk. "You need to take it easy."

I open the trunk, and he puts his bag on top of the spare tire. He brushes the lip of the trunk's hood with his hands. It's rusting. Cars like this weren't made for harsh winters. When I was younger, before we painted the exterior candy apple, we sanded all of the rust away together. He would say, "A little tough love, and she'll be good as new." But now the rust is taking over the body again, slowly but surely.

"I'll ride bitch," Sasha says.

She gets in and slides across the white vinyl seat to the middle. I start the car and crank the heat to high. My father slides in the passenger side and leans his head against the window. I start the car and pull out of the hospital parking lot.

"I've missed you," he says softly.

I can't tell if he is talking to me or to the Falcon. Sasha sits with her legs spread over the center console, one leg touching mine, the other close to my father's. After a couple minutes of silence, I punch the buttons on the radio and watch the dial spring back and forth through static. I land on an oldies song and leave it. My father hums along softly.

"Your grandpa used to play this all the time," he says.

"I like your car, Mr. Miller," Sasha says. She talks to him like the orderlies talk to my grandmother at the nursing home. Like he's a child.

"It was your grandfather's pride and joy," my father says to me. "When I'm gone, it will go to you." He wipes his forehead and turns the ivory heat dial to *off*.

"When did you lose him?" Sasha asks.

"A long time ago, before you were born, kiddo."

"Sorry to hear that. How did he die?"

I can tell she isn't used to people ignoring her, and she isn't about to let my father deprive her of a real story. My father moves close to the window slowly, his head turned away from us.

"He started the Falcon in the garage," he says, "and didn't open the garage door."

I glance at my father. I can tell he's uncomfortable because his knee shakes, and he cracks his knuckles. Sasha is pushing him. She wants to see if he is breakable. Part of me wants to know, too. But the way he tugs at his plastic bracelet and leans against the fogging window glass tells me it hurts.

"He wasn't well," I say and pinch her thigh.

"Jesus," Sasha says.

Just then, we pass through more meadowlarks. One nearly hits the windshield. I swerve a little. Sasha screams.

"Damn birds all over the highway," my father says. "Don't they have the sense to head south?"

The birds disappear in a cloud of snow behind the Falcon. The endless snow-covered fields are going gray as the sun falls.

"I can hardly get a word out of your daughter about her mother, Mr. Miller," Sasha says. "Where did you two meet?"

I can feel my father shuffle in his seat.

"I met her at a bar somewhere near here," he says. "She was the bartender, and I was—"

"The pool tournament champ," I say.

"Did you know the minute you saw her?" Sasha asks. "Sappy romance novel and all that?"

I glance at him, wanting desperately to see his reaction. My father nods once and softly runs his fingernail across the window, small shards of frost falling into his lap.

"Did people treat you poorly because you were different?"

"Sasha," I say, my voice louder than I intend.

"People say what they want," my father says. "Didn't affect me."

He speaks clearly now, and I can feel him looking at me. My grandmother used to say leaving was in my mother's DNA, that all Arapaho people are born with natural wanderlust given to them through ancestors who followed herds around the prairie. My mother left when I was three. I have a picture of her in my mind, but nothing else. She has a strong chin, dark flowing hair, almond eyes. My father always said she was wild from the beginning—stealing, raising hell in the Falcon. I used to tell myself she was kidnapped by cowboys. I glance at my reflection in the rearview mirror and don't see the beautiful Arapaho woman from my imagination. I see my father's pale skin.

"I'm tired," my father mumbles and tells me to wake him when we get to a good place to eat.

Sasha moves close to me. "He seems harmless to me," she whispers.

Massive dark clouds gather, stretching across the prairie, casting the fields, like moors, in shadow. We drive in silence as the wind picks up and yesterday's snowfall starts to blow, covering the countryside in a thin, white veil.

"Are you going to miss this?" Sasha asks.

I can feel her play with my hair again. She starts slowly, waiting to see if I will stop her. I let her this time; my father is asleep on the other side of the car. I picture us together on the beach in California. The sun sets just like it does on the Malibu postcard she stole. We share a towel under a palm tree. There are people like us, happy and sharing towels, building castles. The sand is warm beneath our bodies, and the air is moist. I feel lightheaded, scared and excited like I did when I finally said out loud, "I need to get out of here," and Sasha hugged me for the first time and said, "Fuck it, let's go," and I felt her soft body against mine, her hair sticking to the sweat on my neck. I would have told her I loved her right there, but the storefront bell above the door dinged, and the moment passed.

I would trade these dark clouds for green mountains and these fields for golden beaches any day. I shake my head, and we drive in peace for a while until I see a sign with the symbol for food and gas.

"Let's stop at that diner," I say. I need air, and it seems like as good of a place as any to tell my father I am leaving. I don't know how he will react to the idea of living on his own. Perhaps in public, he won't make a scene.

We drive past a church sign that reads: "Prayer is the Best Wireless Connection." Sasha snorts and says, "Amen."

The diner's parking lot is empty except for a couple of semis and a church van. My father shifts in his seat and lifts his head.

"World-famous Sour Cream and Raisin Pie," he reads on the diner window.

We cruise past a hand-painted mural of Santa serving pie and find a parking spot close to the door. My father urges us not to slam the doors when we get out. We walk through a wooden archway covered with dusty plastic ivy. Shelves with antique teacups and Norman Rockwell tin paintings cover the soft gray-and-white-checkered walls. Sasha chooses an empty booth by a window with a white plastic tablecloth. It is close to a bar-style counter, and in a revolving case at the end, there are three pies glistening in the fluorescent light. A sign above the window is written in loopy black calligraphy. It reads: "Home is where the heart is." The paint is cracked. She slides in first, and I sit next to her. Our legs touch. Her naked arms are warm against mine.

My father sits across from us. "Is that a tattoo?" he asks Sasha.

Sasha tugs at the neck of her shirt and reveals a small shamrock. "My first," she says. "I'm 100 percent Irish."

A cherubic waitress approaches our booth. She wears the cliché diner staff uniform—polka-dotted dress, black and white saddle shoes. She has a pin on her apron with a picture of two overweight pugs that reads: "Pugs and Kisses."

"What can I get for you?" she asks. We order three cheeseburgers and Cokes. The waitress puts her pen behind one ear and leaves.

"What does your father do?" my father asks Sasha. He avoids looking at her directly for too long, like she's the sun. But at least he isn't ignoring her anymore.

"My dad's an engineer," she says. "He develops technology that they use in space. My grandfather was an engineer, too."

This is a lie, but I let her tell it. I try to imagine being her. Beautiful, outspoken.

"Fixing's in your blood," my father says. He taps his fingers on the windowsill for a moment, then studies the caulking.

"Isn't that great, Dad?" I ask.

He doesn't respond. He has bags under his eyes, and his mouth hangs open slightly.

"What are you doing?" I ask, nudging him under the table.

"Nothing, kiddo." He snaps out of his daze.

"Is it the meds?" Sasha asks.

He blushes and shrugs. I wonder if he will be okay on his own. I try not to think about it.

"I'm going to the bathroom," I say. I look over my shoulder. My father runs his thumb along the window's seal again.

"I'll come with you," Sasha says. We pass a table packed with kids who appear to be on a youth group trip. They are blowing straw wrappers at one another and laughing.

"What time is it?" I ask Sasha when we enter the ladies' room. There are three stalls, one without a door, and a window, open a crack.

"I don't know, getting late. Your father seems okay. I know a guy who was on meds for a while and—"

"Your uncle?"

"Hey. That was true."

"My father's schizophrenic," I say, "and so was my grandfather." And one day, it could be me. I search Sasha's face for any sign of fear. This is her out. "Do you still want to leave with me?" I ask.

Sasha takes cigarettes out of her purse and taps the pack gently. I look out the window. The snow has started to fall and the wind forces snowy pines to shift. I pull the window closed and lock it. And then check the lock.

"Hey," Sasha says and moves close to me. I feel her hand against my back. "You'll be fine."

Her hand is warm. Goosebumps creep up my neck. She hugs me, and I feel her chest against mine. Every place she touches tingles. After a minute, she pulls away and slides two cigarettes between her lips and lights them. After the ends burn and glow red, she hands me one. I watch her take another drag, and then she applies more lipstick in the mirror. I mimic her movement. For a moment, I don't see my reflection anymore. I am a beautiful Arapaho woman with flowing dark hair and skin like rich soil.

"Relax," she says, pursing her lips. "Your makeup is running." She licks her thumb and wipes my cheek with her wet finger. She kisses me; her lip ring is cool against my skin. I can almost hear the ocean waves rolling in and out, and I can smell the sea-salt air.

Just then, the bathroom door swings open. I pull away from Sasha. The "Pugs and Kisses" waitress stands in the doorway, her apron stained with ketchup. I tuck my unkempt hair behind my ears.

"Can we help you?" Sasha asks. She takes a long drag of her cigarette. The waitress' eyes narrow. She shakes her head, but says nothing and backs out the way she came.

"We should go," I say.

My face is hot. Sasha throws her cigarette out the window. We pass the front counter, and I notice the waitress talking to the cook in a hushed voice, watching us as we head back to the booth. The food is at the table, and my father is almost done with his burger. I slide in close to Sasha.

"Where you been?" he asks. "Food's getting cold."

Before I can reply, the waitress approaches our booth.

"Hey," my father tells her, "can we get a slice of that world-famous sour cream and raisin pie?" My dad seems in better spirits.

"We're out," the waitress says, scratching her taut brown bun with her pencil.

"You mean that case over there on the counter is full of nothing?"

The waitress shifts her weight to one hip and avoids my father's eyes. "Look, sir, we don't want any trouble," she says. I can see the cook. He listens in the kitchen door, his burly arms crossed. "We got a van of church kids over there. We think you should all head out." The waitress looks at Sasha and me.

My shoulders ache. Sasha looks at her lap, quiet now. The muscles around my father's mouth tremble.

"Let's just go," I say, inching toward the edge of the booth.

"You got a problem?" My father throws his napkin on his plate of uneaten fries.

The waitress backs up a little and says, "I'll call the sheriff. We have the right to refuse service to anyone." The waitress shuffles back to the kitchen for the phone; the cook follows.

"Dad," I start to say. But he gets up from the booth.

"We're leaving," he says, "but before we do, we're taking a pie for the road." My father heads to the counter, and takes a pie from the revolving case. For a moment, I see blue and red flashing lights. We need to leave. I pull Sasha toward the door, keys in hand. My father follows.

We slam our doors, and I drive away, gripping the steering wheel. We drive in silence, no questions from Sasha, no music, nothing.

"That's just like these smalltown ignoramuses to have a problem with the mentally ill," my father finally says. "Must have seen my bracelet." He tugs hard at the plastic. It snaps in two.

I take a long breath. "Dumb hicks," I say.

"That was incredible, Mr. Miller," Sasha says, a small tremble in her voice.

I glance over to see him smile. I think he feels like a hero for the first time in a while. I can feel myself growing calmer. The more road between that place and us, the better. Sasha and my father share the sour cream and raisin pie, eating it like children, scooping it up with their fingers. I'm not hungry.

After twenty or so miles, Sasha, content and full of pie, falls asleep on my shoulder. The complete pitch darkness of the prairie reminds me of waiting to see my father when he got home late from work. When he worked construction in the winter, when farming was slow, he didn't get home until after my grandmother put me to bed. When the prairie winds rapped at the windows of our farmhouse. I pressed my face against the frosted window, waiting to see the Falcon's lights at the end of our driveway.

My father whispers from the passenger seat, "I'm sorry I'm all you've got."

I look over. I can barely see his face in dark, but something in his voice tells me he's sincere. "It's okay."

"I want you to know I'm sorry for disappearing on you. Doing things like this with you, well, reminds me of being with your mother."

I pull my dark hair to one side. "You should know why we got kicked out of there," I say. "It's because the waitress saw Sasha and me together—"

"When we get home, things will go back to the way they were," my father says.

I imagine going back to the farmhouse. The grandfather clocks, the rock-bedded garage, the tire swing by the woodpile. The overgrown hay fields, the sunflowers hanging low. The thought of going back there makes me feel drained, bloodless. I think this is the moment. I should tell him now that I'm not coming home.

But the snowflakes fall and melt almost as soon as they hit the windshield, and I don't say a word. I'll leave in the morning. He'll figure it out. He'll find my clothes and my suitcase gone. Imagining my father finding my hollow closet and empty bed isn't what makes me shudder. It's that I'm able to go so easily. Like cutting my long, dark braided hair with one snip.

I brush my lips against Sasha's forehead, while she rests on my shoulder. I look over at my father; he's asleep now and snoring. His head rests on the white vinyl seat. I try to make out the image of the paradise postcard. It hangs from the visor a foot from my father's face. Cruising through the darkness of the prairie, with the dim light of the Falcon's radio, I can see a palm tree and maybe some sand, but just barely.

Coralee Robbins Mafficks the Fall of Art

Amy Wright

Coralee dusts roadsides with lupines, coos bless yous
from clawfoot bathtubs, heron-blue handkerchief
raising passing fishermen.

                She drawls, bottom lip a curl
                      of baler twine,
rear-ends a Civic at the Jefferson yield sign,

weeps, circles
lakes and pulpits, strings butterfly lights
from camper awnings, howls

over slick-glazed, sweet-sauced carcasses,
dabs her fingertips with Wetnaps,
communing foremost with the holy
mackerels of deliciousness.

BIRCH STREET

Charles P. Ries

Sitting on the porch outside my walk-up with Elaine,
watching the Friday night action on Birch Street.
Southside's so humid the air weeps.

Elaine and I are weeping, too.
Silent tears of solidarity.
She's so full of Prozac she can't sleep, and
I'm so drunk I can't think straight.
Her depression and my beer free our tears
from the jail we carry in our hearts.

Neighbors and strangers pass by in the water vapor.
Walking in twos and fours. Driving by in suped-up
cars and wrecks. Skinny, greased-up gangbangers
with pants so big they sweep the street, and girlfriends
in dresses so tight they burn my eyes.

I can smell Miguel's Taco Stand. Hear the cool
Mexican music he plays. Sometimes I wish Elaine
were Mexican. Hot, sweet, and the ruler of my passion;
but she's from North Dakota, a silent state where
you drink to feel and dance and cry.

Sailing, drifting down Birch Street. Misty boats,
street shufflers, and señoritas. Off to their somewhere.
I contemplate how empty my can of beer is and
how long I can live with a woman who cries all day.

Mondays are better. I sober up and lay lines for the
gas company. Good, clean work. Work that gives me
time to think about moving to that little town in central
Mexico I visited twenty years ago, before Birch Street,
Elaine, and three kids nailed my ass to this porch.

STOOP

Alexa Mergen

Desperation nipped at Ben's heels like a cattle dog. Iris had no idea how in hock they were. He could not tell her. After all, he had promised to take care of her. He had taken her away from her parents' twelfth-floor apartment, lined with black lacquered shelves heavy with books and silver candlesticks that—Iris' mother, Annabelle, informed him on his first visit, placing one like a weapon into his sweaty, callused palm while he shifted like a nervous horse standing in the hall—had been in her family since her ancestor, John Plane, sailed up the Rappahannock River in 1717, with soapstone sculptures Frank Collins collected on treks to the Arctic, Central America, Africa, places he had lectured as a professor of the study of man. When Ben Tattel, by some dumb luck, collected this finishing-school beauty from her apartment and married her, brought her, he thought, like a fairytale princess to the forest in the city, he promised that, though she would not be rich, she would always be safe. He considered his wife fragile and cherished her innocence. He wanted her to be happy.

Friday night, when Iris suggested over a dinner, just the two of them, Abel and Cici off with their friends, that he ask his sister to pay him for his share of their parents' house, his first impulse was to saddle Moss, the quarter horse mare he had not ridden in months, and keep riding along the river until he reached the Chesapeake Bay. By horseback, though, even in 1981, that would be a journey of days, the way blocked by highways, houses, and bridges. There was no room anymore for creatures afoot. Maybe that was the problem. People took the new subway (his father would have been dumbfounded by that system, and the rats its construction stirred up), buses, and drove their cars, even with the price of gas creeping up. And they rode bicycles, like his own son, Abel, who preferred a bike to the horses they had at Tangle Creek City Stable. Ben's second impulse was to go to the boat. This he did on Saturday morning. He could think when he was walking, on a horse, or on the water. Movement made him aware of the future and the past and emboldened him to move forward.

Zach's Boat House was tucked under the Whitehurst Freeway near Key Bridge. Ben kept a canoe there that his father had christened the *Durham*, named for the type of vessel George Washington used to cross the Delaware River in 1776. Ben's *Durham* was a simple plank canoe, painted the creamy white of mock-orange flowers. His father had been barred from military service during the Second World War due to a severe limp, a legacy of childhood polio. The man had trained as a plumber, joking, *You spend most of your time on your back reaching up. Not much need for the legs,* and an amateur woodworker. On land, Ben and his sister, Bebe, often waited for their father to catch up to them, embarrassed by his loping gait when other fathers strode steadily. But on the river, Patrick Tattel moved the balanced boat with grace, dipping the birch paddle noiselessly. On the river, you could remember that everything in life begins with making something, whether it's a pie, like Bebe made with their mother, Marie, or a boat, or a business, like Patrick did with Tattel Plumbing. *Make something of yourself. Make something of yourself.* Patrick always delivered the command twice in a row, once for each child. And then, a third time, *Make something of yourself.* A charm. Bebe repeated the phrase three times in a whisper to her doll, curled up on an old patio cushion in the center of the canoe. Ben was placed in the bow, and his father's voice from the stern pushed him on.

The only print Patrick Tattel read was daily papers, the *Post* and the *Star*, but he could read water, whether it was gurgling up through a tub drain or flowing toward the sea. Much of his job was routine, Patrick told twelve-year-old Ben, as they glued strips of marine plywood into place along the boat's frame: the routine was clogged commodes, stopped-up sinks, tree roots in sewer lines—but river water told a new story every day. It was like the hymns they sang at St. Peter's: though the words never varied, changing voices altered the resulting sound from Sunday to Sunday.

Ben's truck was the only vehicle parked on the shoulder of the road by the boat house. Thin sheets of ice floated in the Potomac River and huddled against the bank of Roosevelt Island, on the far side. If he were a younger man, Ben would have lifted the boat from the rack—space 22, a paddle balanced on the thwarts—and put in anyway. It always cheered him to see how the boat found her center as she bounced up after being set in the water for adventure.

But today, he needed solutions, not adventure. He needed money.

Ben unlocked and slid open the boathouse door. The rowing shells, canoes, and kayaks waited in darkness like the crocus and tulip bulbs Iris dug into the soil, rich with their own horses' manure, that bloomed midspring to form elaborate patterns of color that she called her "Turkish carpet." Thinking of these flowers brought Ben a tremor of hope. They still had six horses. Between his daughter Cici and himself, maybe they could manage without hiring more help in the stable. He would just have to get used to a shovel again.

With bare hands, Ben brushed cobwebs from the *Durham*. He used his sleeve to burnish the brass nameplate. When Iris' flowers bloomed, he promised himself, he would get Abel and Cici back on the river, the three of them, like they used to do when the kids were small. And today, he would ask Bebe for his share of the money from the house. It was all they had been left by their parents.

It seemed long ago, now. When Marie got sick, Patrick stayed home more and more, holding her hand. She wanted to be read to from collections of *Ripley's Believe It or Not*. Facts weird and true calmed her: that fruit-bat soup was a delicacy in Palau, or a woman survived a fall from the 86th floor of the Empire State Building, or a cat in England can purr as loud as a motorcycle. There were hundreds of thousands of facts, enough to read for hours on end, to speculate on. Immobilized, wasting, she could suspend her belief and swallow novelty, even if she could not suspend her pain and swallow soup. These random oddities bound Patrick and Marie like superglue. Bebe took to bringing her parents a tray, usually homemade pie and lemonade, both of which her mother had taught her to make.

Gradually, the business of Tattel Plumbing faded along with the lettering on the side of Patrick's truck, left parked in the sun so long that city traffic enforcers fitted the front tire with a yellow boot. Ben had to walk to the police station and pay the fine with money saved from mowing lawns. Marie died after four years of suffering, years of midnight trips to Providence Hospital, and long days when Bebe and Ben sat opposite each other on the front stoop playing jacks, scared to go to the park that their mother might die when they left, and they would miss saying goodbye.

They were outside when Marie and Patrick died within the same hour, when Ben was fifteen and Bebe, twelve. The coroner's report said congestive heart failure for Marie and stroke for Patrick. Patrick had left the paperwork for a life-insurance policy in plain view on the dresser. The children received a thousand dollars in cash and the house fully paid. Ben lied to the medics who came in an ambulance to take the bodies away, saying his uncle was coming to stay. It did not seem like a lie, as the day felt ordinary. The ambulance did not sound its siren. The children had for a long time fended for themselves. Patrick's brother, Chad, did arrive at Union Station with his overnight kit in a grocery bag. He slept on the couch for six nights. He paid for plots at Tangle Creek Cemetery and headstones with stacks of dollar bills rolled with a rubber band. He even stood by the children as a priest said the right words to make Patrick and Marie rest in heaven. Then, Chad Tattel lied to the priest and said he would stay with the kids, while Ben and Bebe watched. When he left the children by the red, white, and blue bus stop, pressing a five-dollar bill in each child's hand, and walked away to catch the train, the brother and sister decided to go to Roy Rogers for roast beef and fries. They were suddenly very hungry. And in no hurry to get home.

On that cool fall day, no one else attended the funeral service. The leaves of the trees of Tangle Creek Park caught the golden sunlight and held onto it greedily. The Tattels' friends had faded away when Patrick stopped answering the door or opening the curtains. Some neighbors wondered if the house were unoccupied. They paid little attention to two children living alone. Ben dropped out of high school, ducking the truancy officer for a couple of weeks, then went to work at the stable, a few times sleeping in the barn to avoid his sister's repeated inquiry, *Are you okay?* Bebe finished high school, babysitting evenings and weekends, then married the first boy she kissed. All that was a long time ago, Ben thought. He had been good to his sister, as he had promised. The siblings could work something fair. Ben knocked on the *Durham's* gunwale for luck and locked the boat safely.

Traffic was light. Ben reached the old row house after just two songs on the radio and the hourly news summary. As he parked, he noticed paint peeling from the bricks, the front gate leaning on its hinges, plastic wrap tacked in the windows to keep out drafts. The house had been white for as long as he could remember, until a few years ago, when Bebe had it painted rose red and green. As more and more people bought up the historic houses and redid them in subdued shades of gray and beige, Bebe's stood out like a schoolgirl whose clothes are not quite right.

When he approached the iron steps to Bebe's front door, Ben's resolve wavered. He conceived of life as an obstinate horse that, if controlled with clear authority, had no need for cruelty. Right now, he was not sure what the command was. He wanted to shake the lead rope and tell life to back up.

"Ben! Are you okay?" Bebe cried, wiping her hands on her apron. "I saw your truck pull up. I've been baking, don't you know? You wouldn't believe what some of these new neighbors will pay for a pie, Ben. I can hardly keep up. They love to have parties. Oscar Brown, next door, he squeezed 200 people into his backyard, and it's not any bigger than ours. He ordered 20 shepherd's pies and 25 fruit." She descended each step haltingly, pinching her eyes. "It's these knees," she explained. "Just like Mom, remember? Poor thing." In imitation of Bebe, the four following children stepped and stopped behind their mother. "I'm not sick, though," she added hastily.

"Henry around?" Ben asked.

Bebe shook her head, and the eldest boy looked at his mother. Ben remembered that the boy was born around the time of Jimmy Carter's inauguration, so he must be about four. That boy held the littlest, who was born on Lincoln's birthday, a year ago. From her hospital bed, Bebe had told her big brother that the auspicious date was a sign that her youngest would be an important politician. She even named him Lincoln. Henry, who Ben suspected drank too much, seemed dazed the day of Lincoln's birth and merely nodded as the nurse filled in the certificate. Why would he object? His parents had named him Henry Ford. It struck Ben as he watched the details of a new life being logged, how people carry papers, like horses do, and cannot escape those first definitions. The baby would forever be Lincoln Ford. It sounded like a car dealership.

The oldest was called Scott. Ben and Iris were his godparents, though he had to admit, they had not done much about it. The two girls were Stacy and Shelly, but he was not sure which was which. Bebe finally reached the brick path.

"It's a good thing I canned peaches and strawberries last summer," she said. "It was plenty hot in that steamy kitchen last August, but Henry gets the bruised fruit for next to nothing. And Oscar said the pies tasted like the ones his mama used to make. That's high praise. He said, 'Bee'— he calls me Bee, which I don't mind; I'm surely busy as a bee." She stopped to laugh at her own joke. "'Bee,' he says, 'you can expect many more pie orders from me.'" She took Lincoln in one arm from Scott, who handed the baby over willingly, and said quickly, "Scoot, Scott. Take the girls in for me." She placed her other hand on Ben's arm and lowered her voice. "It's a good thing, Ben, that I am earning pin money from those pies. We're stretched thin as a sheet of strudel dough."

Ben did not know how thin strudel dough was, but her meaning was clear. He ran a hand through his hair. "I'm sorry to hear that, Bebe."

She sat down on the step. Cici had told her aunt last summer when she was over helping with canning that siblings share more genes with each other than with either of their birth parents. *How can Abel and I be so different, then?* Cici had asked her aunt over the sound of boiling water, holding her sad face in her hands, surrounded by jars of gold and red where the girl sat at the kitchen table.

Bebe patted the step for Ben to sit beside her. "What brings you over our way, Ben?" she asked, holding the baby's arms and gently making him clap. Lincoln opened his lips in a gummy smile.

"Oh." It felt good to sit on the stoop with his sister again, to feel the cold rise up through his pant legs from the iron step.

"Look at that robin. So early," Bebe exclaimed. "They nest in that silver maple every year."

Ben heard his mother's voice surfacing from the furthest corner of his brain where he stored geometry formulas and snippets of songs from the 60s. *Beatrice walks on the sunny side of the street*, she said. And his father's voice, closer, ringing like tinnitus: *Take care of your sister.*

"Bebe," Ben said, "I was just passing by and thought how long it's been since I saw the little one." He took Lincoln on his lap to hold him close, then wrapped the baby warmly with his own soft muffler.

MOB OF ONE

Normal

maybe
they don't express these things
the rye the whiskey the screaming
in the hall—the piss in front
of the door—the backhand
slapping like an angry
spanish dance
across the cheek
of a child.

every girl
holds at least
one secret
out in her palm
far from the crowd
in her own private world
in her own mob of one.

every girl
knows the land of the turtle
the language of the sickly
the chambers of the swan.
every girl
rallies a flower
discovers a feather
champions a stone
she protects from the world.

maybe
there is no word left
to express the sound
of a siren shattering the moon—
no lighthouse bright enough
to guide your tiny vessel
out of the harbor of tears &
into the sea of an
unforgiving sorrow. maybe
there is no one left to blame.

maybe
there is no expression left
no words left
to the song you have not
written yet
that carries on its wings
a hope
that sings
your name.

SCULPTING SAND

Steve Karas

It's just past noon, and I see Casey is finally awake. He's wearing his tie-dyed T-shirt, eying us from the edge of the beach, sipping on what I assume are two fingers of whiskey from a Styrofoam cup. My wife, Sharon, is beside me, kneeling under the shade of the umbrella. She's sculpting a sandcastle for little Millie who's walking back and forth from the ocean, dumping and refilling her pail.

A young family from upstate New York has returned from lunch and is making camp next to us. They're renting a beachside cottage for the week, too. Their three-year-old stomps through the sand to Millie. Their girl's a walking billboard for Disney in her princess swimsuit, arm floaties, and hat. Sharon and I register these things, these little details, because it's been so many years since we've had to raise a toddler of our own, and I know Sharon is beating herself up for not dressing Millie in a princess suit.

The New Yorker lumbers over to me, a breeze lifting his unbuttoned Cuban shirt and exposing his burnt torso. I glance at his wife rubbing lotion into her thighs, her beach chair positioned to face the sun. I wish I were thirty again.

"So what do you do up there in the Empire State?" I ask him.

"I'm a therapist."

"How about that. You think I can book a session for my son?" I gesture toward Casey, only half-kidding.

The New Yorker's daughter is pulling sand toys out of Millie's basket, even from her hands. "Don't just take things from her," he tells her. "Ask her nicely." But Millie obliges, has no problem sharing, keeps digging. "What an even-tempered little girl," he says.

I wonder if I should tell him, if it's too much information, but I say it anyway. "She has a heart defect, so she's always been pretty subdued. Tires easily."

He shoots me a sympathetic glance, doesn't say much. Most people don't know how to respond, even shrinks, maybe.

"The doctors were ready to operate when she was born," I say, "but she came out healthy. A miracle, really. The problem is her body is getting too big now for her heart."

He nods his head, tells me he's sorry, and then stares across the horizon. I spare him the specifics. That she has L-Transposition of the great arteries, a large VSD, pulmonary stenosis, and constrictions in her heart's blood vessel. "How 'bout a beer?" I ask him. "Or a bourbon?"

He declines.

It's not that I care, because I couldn't give two shits, but I'm curious what he's thinking. I'm often curious what people are thinking when they see Sharon and me with Millie. Especially when they find out she has a heart problem. I look at the shrink, eyes hidden behind his aviator shades, and I wonder if he's blaming us. If he's surmising we're two irresponsible old fuckers who decided to have a kid at our age. It doesn't take a shrink, though, to understand you never know what the story is behind closed doors.

Casey and I are walking along the shore, under a cloudless sky and an unyielding sun. I'm pulling Millie along in her red wagon. My sandals sink into the powdery sand with each step.

"So tell me about Utah?" I say.

"I'd rather not talk about it right now."

"I paid thirty-thousand dollars to send you there. I saved you from getting locked up for half a year. Don't you think I deserve to know how it went?"

"I said I don't want to talk about it," Casey says. His hair falls over his brow and he flicks his head, this annoying head flick he and all his friends do.

There are happy couples walking by us, families, sunbathers and joggers all around, too, so I don't press him any further. "Okay, all right."

Casey has spent the last two months in a wilderness camp after a string of run-ins with the Menasha Police. Possession of marijuana with the intent to sell (he swore he was just smoking with Hannah, his on-again / off-again girlfriend, and the little extra bag they had in the car was only for them), possession of stolen property (cash taken from area vending machines by a friend who owed him for reasons we could assume), and possession of marijuana while on probation. The police have come to know Casey well, have had it out for him, I think. It's a small town we live in, only about 17,000 people. One of the Fox Cities in eastern Wisconsin running along the banks of the Fox River. The police don't have a whole lot to do there and, in fairness, neither do the kids.

"Have you heard from Hannah?" I ask him.

"Yeah, she says she has a lawyer. Supposedly, she's got a job now, doing better. She's going to try to get custody."

Seagulls circle overhead, eying picnic spreads. Millie sings Disney songs to herself from the wagon. We start heading up toward the low-rise condos dotting the beach, painted in calming pastels. Salmon, cream, peach.

"Let's just get through Millie's surgery next month," I say. "We've always said you and Hannah are her rightful mom and dad, so that would be the goal." This is the message I've been repeating to myself for three years.

My mother is sitting in a beach chair, protected by the shade of the cottage, and sipping on a Manhattan. I convinced her to join us on this trip. Thought it'd be good for her. For Casey, too. Having his granny with him, reminding him who he is deep down under the layers of regret and failed dreams.

"Hi, Mom." She doesn't hear me. Has no idea what we've been through the last couple years or where Casey has been for the past two months. As far as she knows, he's a typical twenty-year-old, slogging through college courses and hanging out with pals. She brags about him to her friends because people only see what they want to.

"Why don't we go in for lunch?" I tell Casey.

"I'll be there in a minute."

He stays outside to have a cigarette while I pull Millie out of the wagon and carry her into the cottage.

Millie is napping. Casey is, too. Sharon and I sit in the kitchen, talking quietly over the whir of the tropical ceiling fan. The lime-green walls are covered in ceramic starfish and crabs and a wooden sign with a painting of a margarita glass that reads: "What Happens at the Beach, Stays at the Beach."

"He doesn't want to accept any responsibility for her," Sharon says. "He acts like she's not even his."

"Let's give them some time together. Maybe this week will do them good."

"Utah hasn't changed him at all. And you've been bending over backward for him."

She says it like it's a bad thing, me trying to keep our kid from sinking, from getting swallowed up by earth. She's already given me a hard time about hiring him as a receptionist at my law office and setting up an apprenticeship with a Fox Cities real estate big shot. I'm paying Casey's salary with the guy, though Casey's not aware of that. I know there's a fine line between helping and enabling. I understand that, but every father wants to see his son become a man.

I tell Sharon about Hannah. About her wanting custody. Her eyes get wide. She puts her hand over her mouth, stands up to give her something to do other than cry. Because of Millie's heart and Hannah's drug use and emotional problems, we've had custody of Millie since the day she was born. At first, it was just to protect her, give her a chance at life. We said if the kids ever got their shit together, we'd give Millie back to them, her rightful parents. It's hard not to feel like she's ours now, though, with everything we've sacrificed, how much our life has changed. For the better in a lot of ways. Sharon had to give up her career as a stone sculptor to take care of Millie. She misses it every day, but if it's between sculpting and Millie, there's no competition. After three years, we feel like she deserves nothing less than what we've been giving her.

"She can't even take care of herself, and she thinks she can take care of a child?" Sharon says to no one in particular.

"He says she's getting her life together."

"She still smokes around Millie. Even with her heart problems."

These are all things I know well, but I nod my head anyway. I get up to pour myself a bourbon.

"What did we do wrong?" Sharon asks.

"Maybe we were too hard on him growing up."

"Or maybe we were too easy."

Sharon and I smoked plenty of pot when we were Casey's age. We named him after the Grateful Dead song that was playing when we met, for God's sake, but we ended up being productive adults, law-abiding citizens. I've told Casey, but should I have? It was more cautionary than anything like, *Look, we were teenagers once, too, and we know you're going to drink and we know you're going to smoke a little weed, but be careful. Be smart. This isn't your father's weed. It's a hell of a lot more potent these days, more addictive.* Who knows, maybe it kept him from moving on to harder stuff. Parenting is full of second-guessing. Even the New Yorker will see that someday.

"We've always known this was a possibility," I tell Sharon. "We've always said they're the rightful parents. We just need to get through the surgery."

In the monitor, we see Millie moving in her bed. Sharon goes in, brushes her hair from her face, and kisses her forehead. I check on Casey in the next room and he's lying face up, not moving, like a corpse. The bed sheets smell like cigarette smoke. I put my hand to his chest to see if I can feel it rise and fall, to make sure he's alive. He lets out a deep breath that startles me. I cover him with the sheet and tiptoe back out.

The sun is beginning to set, and fishermen and seagulls have taken over the beach. We're on a dolphin cruise of the upper Boca Ciega Bay, sailing past mangrove islands and million-dollar homes. Beer and hotdogs are being served from a cooler out of the front of the catamaran. We're fifteen minutes in and have already seen two bottlenose dolphins leap from the water. Millie's joy—seeing dolphins for the first time and jumping up, no less—is worth the fourteen-hundred miles we've traveled.

The tour guide announces over the mic that a dolphin is riding the bow wave of the boat, and passengers stand up, pull out their cameras, start taking video. Casey picks Millie up and takes her to see. They're hanging over the edge of the boat.

"Be careful," Sharon says to him. "It's bumpy."

"Let 'em be," I say.

Millie is squealing in delight, the wind blowing her hair back. It pushes her hat right off her head. Sharon and I look at each other and are both thinking the same thing. Casey is on his second beer and who knows how much booze he had this morning, how much is still in his system. By instinct, my eyes locate the hook ladder and life rings.

"She's fine," I tell Sharon and force a smile.

Casey is laughing, too, and I see a glimpse of the old version of him, before the Phish tours and tie-dyed T-shirts, before the long hair and the head flicking. A thought pops into my mind, this horrible thought, that the birth of Millie ruined his life. Maybe he would have gone down a normal path if he hadn't had to deal with becoming a father at seventeen, the father of a sick kid, at that. Was he getting high to escape, to forget about the fact his life was irreversibly changed?

Casey looks at us, still smiling, and shakes his head like he can see the dread in our eyes, the distrust, trying to tell us, *You two are over the top. Stop worrying so much. I'm going to be okay this time.*

"Dolphin, dolphin!" Millie screams, alternating between turning away scared and leaning back over the edge to get another look.

The next morning, I sit on the balcony and have my morning coffee. The windchimes jingle. A brown anole lizard scales the wall. It's another day of hoping the rising ocean sun will thaw our hearts before the Wisconsin snow has even had a chance to thaw itself.

By nine, the kids are still asleep. My mom is in the family room watching game shows on TV. Sharon and I decide to go to the local Publix to stock up.

"Be back soon, Mom," I say.

When we return, my mom is still in front of the TV, but Millie and Casey are nowhere to be found. Their empty cereal bowls are in the sink, their flip-flops gone.

"Hey, Mom, where are the kids?" Sharon asks.

"They were just here. Aren't they here?" She's got a mimosa in front of her, and I wonder if she's smashed already.

It's not even noon, so Casey being awake, let alone out of the house, is suspicious. And Millie is a creature of habit. She likes her thirty minutes of Disney cartoons on the iPad before starting the day. Sharon calls Casey's phone, but it goes straight to his voicemail.

"They probably went down to the beach," I say.

The New Yorkers are there. The man is setting up their umbrella, the woman basting their daughter in sunscreen. The sand sculptures Sharon built for Millie the day before have melted back into the ground and are nothing more than mounds. I don't see Casey or Millie anywhere.

"Good morning," they say.

"Good morning. Have you seen our brood, by chance?" I ask.

"No, haven't seen them," the man says. "Not down here."

A little panic starts to set in. I can see it in Sharon's face, too. Fear something terrible has happened. Maybe Millie's been kidnapped by Casey; maybe Hannah is in on it, as well. We've let our guard down too much. I've let my guard down and have fallen victim to an intricate plan. We'll never see Millie's sweet face again. It's a fear even worse than that of her impending surgery, if that's possible, of her not making it through.

I'm too embarrassed to explain the situation to the New Yorkers, to the shrink. What would I even say? *We can't find our daughter who's really our son's daughter but who's kind of like our own daughter because our son is a druggie and, yeah, by the way, we really fucked up raising him. What do you make of that, doc? What diagnosis do you have for this family dynamic?* I turn and almost trip over the girl's sand toys.

We jump into the minivan, crunch over the seashells for a driveway, and start scouring the town. Sharon isn't talking, just searching out the window, left then right. Not at the playground, not climbing the dolphin statue at the Welcome Center, not feeding the turtles at the nature preserve. We cross the causeway and head out of the tourist territory, get lost among the locals. He wouldn't have gone to score some weed with her, would he have? Past tattoo parlors. Past bait & tackle, ammo, and pawn shops.

"I'm sure it's fine," I say, but Sharon doesn't respond. I know, in her head, she's blaming me—*If something bad happened, I swear*, she's thinking. Blaming me for giving Casey a second chance when tough love should have been the only option. And I think I see what Sharon has been seeing for a while: if we're forced to choose between Casey and Millie at this point, Millie wins.

Then, as we head back over the causeway, down Gulf Boulevard toward the cottage, there they are. Casey and Millie, strolling down the sidewalk, holding hands. Each with an ice-cream cone in the other hand. Millie with chocolate, her favorite, melting down her arm. Casey with what I'm guessing is Rocky Road, his usual pick.

Sharon and I look at each other, not with a smirk, but like we've caught ourselves being foolish, because, really, who would feel any different in our position? We step out of the car and approach them.

Millie has chocolate circling her mouth. We can scold Casey for not sending us a text message letting us know where they went or for giving her ice cream before lunch, but we don't. We wouldn't dare.

"Well, hey," Sharon says. "Did you two have fun?" Millie runs into her arms.

I've come to accept that if we're going to make it through this ordeal, it's going to have to be one day at a time. That's what they preach in recovery. And that's what Sharon and I have been telling each other since we found out about Millie's complicated heart. Maybe someday Casey and I will get matching tattoos, father and son, and that's what they'll say. In painful black ink: *One day at a time*.

Baldwin Apples

Sarah Ann Winn

In October, their vinegar
drew bees or decay's sweetening
drew bees. We brought bushel baskets
and sorted. Some for the compost,
the gently bruised for pies. The best,
those half-gone with pocked, perfect skin
still a little green, for canning
and apple butter. The Baldwins
lured me to the kitchen counter.
The turn-and-scraping colander
mill when the cooked apples were poured in—
the splashed juice hot and delicious.
Space made by adding cooked apples
carefully. She tipped the ancient
Dutch oven, and my idea
of plenty poured down. I didn't
dare move or some would go to waste.
Save some for later, she said. Now
we restock the canned-goods cupboard.
No beauty goes to waste here. Fill
the shelf. Put up for lean winter
the sweet of slowly gathering
afternoon, that long fragrant bake,
the whole house cooked up, and browned with
cinnamon. In winter, the sound
of that seal breaking snaps me back
to sorting apples in the sun.
Their scent rolled from Atalanta's
fingers, the breath of Eve before she bit.

Tennessee

Constance Sayers

I had let the seeking of me go on a little too long for everyone's comfort. My name echoed through the yard like a foghorn. The cousins peered up at trees and squeezed themselves under the shrubs attempting to zero in on my hiding place with the precision of a dull-witted infantry armed only with melting popsicles.

Crunched in the backseat of my parents '71 Impala, I ignored them and turned my attention to the book in my hands. While the paper dust-cover claimed it to be Homer, it was actually the Harold Robbins novel hidden underneath that had me transfixed. I had finished the real Homer by the time we reached Cincinnati, and it was now under the floor mat.

Another summer in Tennessee. My father explained he needed to spend time with his family. My mother's side of the family didn't seem to need such keeping. Quietly, she had given up her role as Maggie in the summer regional playhouse production of *Cat on a Hot Tin Roof* to be with us. The playhouse responded quickly by changing their posters with the face of another actress wearing what had been my mother's white slip. As I peered down the hill at the old farmhouse, I thought she had somehow gotten the raw end of the deal.

My book was getting good when I saw two dirty-blond pigtails appear at the car window. I knew they belonged to my cousin, Gertie. Gertie had one of those potbellies that children sometimes have. She was also messy, which meant she was forever spilling things, and her potbelly was catching them. Today, I could tell from the stains on her white tanktop she'd been drinking strawberry Kool-Aid. She put her chin on the open car window and looked at me.

"I found you," she stated.

"Yep." I didn't look up.

"Why are you sitting in here? We were looking for you."

"I'm reading," I said.

"Marcus got tired of looking for you." She paused. "Mom says we *have* to ask you to play with us."

"I don't want to play. I'm reading now." I knew with the arrival of Gertie that what little peace I had enjoyed in the car was about to end. My cousins Marcus, Sara, and Nan swarmed the car, opening all the doors and crawling about the seats like wasps.

"She doesn't want to play," Gertie announced.

"She *can't* play," snapped Marcus. "She's a big baby." He squirmed in his seat and turned to Sara who was positioned at the wheel of the car. "I don't like my seat," he said. "I should drive. Girls can't drive." Marcus had gotten fat since I had seen him last summer. His face was red, and a thin layer of shiny sweat covered his smooth skin. He looked a little like a whale covered in a thin T-shirt.

"Shut up," said Sara, coolly. She began moving the steering wheel back and forth like she was driving. Her brown, Carol Brady shag haircut oddly never moved.

My family didn't live in Tennessee year-round, and this fact bothered Sara. Instead, I arrived every summer, and my grandmother spent more time with me than with the other kids. I'm sure the arrangement seemed equitable to my grandmother since she saw the other kids all year, but it didn't sit well with Sara.

Sara was the self-appointed leader of my cousins' social circle. She was the leader mostly because she would say things the other kids wouldn't, and this raw nerve gave her power. Thinking back on it, I'm sure my cousins were just as afraid that her cruel streak would be turned on them, so they kept her pointed like a dagger right at me.

Not this summer. I was turning twelve, and something had changed in me. Back home in Cleveland, I had started smoking behind the drugstore with my friend, Vera. Vera had hair the color of black licorice that was cut into a sharp bob around her chin. She also went to Catholic school—a mysterious place for a Methodist like me—and her olive legs and yellow plaid school uniform looked downright exotic next to my public-school clothes and pasty, chubby legs.

I didn't enjoy the cigarettes much because I couldn't shake the coughing, so I just gave up and faked it. It was as though I had awakened to the fact I had been assembled and carved out of the sooty streets of Cleveland. As Vera and I stood in the alley with our Virginia Slims between our fingers, I could hear the brakes of the buses grinding and releasing and the screen door of the adjacent diner stretching on its rusty hinges and smacking shut against its frame.

So, this summer, I was more confident than ever that I could handle Sara. I chose my words carefully. "I can do whatever the hell I want to do," I replied.

Sara smiled. She was a master of subtlety. "You swore," she said. "I'm telling Grandma."

I hadn't counted on that comeback, but I couldn't back down now. "Hell if I care," I added.

"Say you're sorry for swearing," Sara demanded from the front seat. "Tell Jesus you're sorry!" She tugged at the steering wheel with both hands. Her head bobbed from side to side like a metronome.

"Yeah," added Marcus. His voice squeaked for a moment, "Say you're sorry." He'd flunked two grades. His mother, my Aunt Betty, liked to say he didn't apply himself in school, but the simple fact was that Marcus was just stupid.

I said nothing.

Finally, Sara spoke. "I'm going to tell Grandma and your mother that you're swearing, and then you'll really get in trouble," she said. Sara and I were now locked in a war of wills. Soon, she recruited one more for her side. "I'll tell Grandma, won't I, Nan?"

Nan knew her cue. Gertie's older sister was normally pleasant, but like some bizarre chemical combination, Nan mixed with Sara produced a treacherous compound. "If Sara won't tell, then I will." Nan folded her arms in front of her.

"My mother won't give a *damn*," I said.

"That's it. I'm telling." Sara slammed the car door and peered into the back seat. Then she ran full speed to my grandmother's house with Marcus, Nan, and Gertie following closely behind her.

I had wanted to stay in Cleveland. I had wanted to walk to the drugstore with Vera and fill up a candy bag filled with Swedish Fish and pumpkin seeds and eat them out of the tiny paper bags at the candy aisle. I hated spending the summer in Tennessee because I'd return in August to find that everything in Cleveland had changed. Vera would have picked up some other vice with a new friend because I never seemed to stay in one place long enough.

Within minutes, I watched my mother walk toward the car. Although her arms swung casually at her side and swept her hips, as a stage actress there was nothing carefree about her walk. I had seen her performance twice during the spring run. She looked different on set with the hot lights and auburn hair dye. She was the only mother I knew who still had long hair. She opened the driver's side door and sat in the seat most recently occupied by Sara.

"She told on me," I said. "I knew it."

"What did you expect?" she said. She turned around to face me and her arm draped the front seat. She looked as though she were about to go on a leisurely drive. "You know they're a bunch of Holy Rollers. Jesus, Maggie."

"They hate me," I replied.

"No, they don't."

I was about to protest when I noticed my mother looking at my book. It dawned on me that the thin Homer dustcover didn't exactly fit her clunky Harold Robbins novel.

"Is that Harold Robbins? What are you doing reading that filth?"

"It's *yours*," I replied, as if that would matter.

She leaned forward to peel the book from my hand. "Go play with your cousins."

"I finished Homer," I said. I wanted her to know that I had done what she'd asked.

My mother's face was stern. "You never finish reading someone as great as Homer," she said. "Read him again."

I didn't want to read Homer again. That was something my father did. He didn't care for the newest writers, the popular artists and musicians that my mother knew. He reread all the books he had read in college. While my mother's book collection expanded to the point she had novels stacked in front of the bookcases, my father's shelf never changed; it simply rotated.

My father taught English. This summer, he had decided to research Tennessee's own short story writer, Peter Taylor, at Sewanee. I tried to act interested in his research because I hoped he'd take me along so I wouldn't get stuck playing with my cousins, but by Kentucky, he'd changed his mind.

My mother fussed with her lipstick in the rearview mirror.

"I'd rather stay here and read," I said.

She sighed deeply and slid her sunglasses down into position on her nose. I sensed a sudden change in her as she looked around the farm. "Margaret, we all have to do things we don't want to do in life. It's about time you got used to it. You need to grow up."

"When are we going home?" I pressed. I meant our Tennessee home, the little cabin about five miles from my grandmother's house. I wouldn't have minded going back to our Cleveland bungalow, either. I tried a new strategy. I would stall her. "Did Tennessee Williams live here?"

She got a wide smile on her face. "No. He grew up in Mississippi, but Noel says his family was from here originally. Just like your father's." She looked directly at me when she spoke her last sentence.

"Will the similarities between us never end?" I rolled my eyes and sank further into my pleather seat.

My mother smiled, and I knew I had softened her. I had noticed recently that she was dropping a new name—"Noel"—into her conversations as if it were a spice she was adding to a dish. This particular "Noel" was the director of the Cleveland Playhouse Theatre where she had worked. He had come to the house for one of her parties at Christmas. He was a wiry chain-smoker with a gravelly voice that he seemed to like to hear, but my mother seemed to find everything he said either "charming" or "fascinating."

We'd all run into Noel at the playhouse when my mother went to pick up her last paycheck. He looked nervous and twitchy when he saw us. He was chewing on a toothpick and kept pulling it out of his mouth and flailing it about like a conductor when he spoke.

"Noel has written a play about Trotsky. Isn't that just fascinating, Gerald?" She poked at my father who was studying the poster of the new actress posing exactly like my mother on the theater sign for *Cat on a Hot Tin Roof*.

"Uh huh," said my father like he'd gotten caught sleeping in class.

My mother glared at him. "Trotsky." And then she sighed. "That is so fascinating."

Now, I let the "l" of Noel roll off of my tongue dramatically. "Did he find another actress to replace you?" As soon as I said it, I could see that she was stung by my question.

"Yes, he did." She slid out of the car and brushed herself off.

"Can we go home now?" I was aware that she was upset about something and that it had to do with Noel and the part of Maggie that she had left back home.

"Not until after we eat." She motioned for me to come out of the car, and we headed down the hill toward the house. As we walked, she pulled me in close to her and then released me.

My grandmother's farm had one of those rare Mail Pouch barns on it. The barn had begun to lean, and she talked a lot about razing it that summer. A moat of lush, purple impatiens surrounded her white farmhouse and extended out around the mailbox to the water well. I could see my grandmother folding a yellow tablecloth over the picnic table as my cousin, Marcus, kicked an orange ball in the field behind the barn. The field was littered with occasional haystacks, not the neat squares we saw in the farms around Cleveland, but the untidy bales that came from old equipment. The red tractor—a relic with a rusted seat—sat next to the doghouse. The dog ran back and forth on a long chain trying to catch Marcus' fly balls.

When I sat down at the table next to my mother, my Aunt Betty was exclaiming how much Nan looked like my mother. I wanted to protest that a resemblance was impossible because my beautiful mother was not even related to Nan by blood, but I ate my hot dog instead and suffered the indignation as Nan preened. In truth, I was hurt that no one thought I looked like my mother. I felt entitled to the resemblance.

My mother smiled sweetly, but I knew she was playing a part. She no more wanted to be in Tennessee than I did.

"So," said my Aunt Betty. "Earl tells me you're acting again." The comment hung in the air for some reason I didn't understand.

My mother looked down at the table and folded her napkin. "I was offered a lead in another Tennessee Williams play directed by a friend of mine," she said. "I turned it down."

"You should be here," said Aunt Betty. "Mother can hardly get around anymore."

My mother smiled at her and picked up my plate, stacking it on top of her own. She walked past Father's empty plate. I watched him duck pitifully to the side for a moment, expecting her to reach around him and pick up his plate, but she never did.

That night, at our rented house, I sat with my mother on the porch swing. I brought out my little blue suitcase packed with my books and papers. My suitcase was the smallest in the set my parents owned. It was a miniature like the ones they carried, and I liked it because it made me feel like I belonged to them.

My mother smiled when she saw that I had packed her old plays. I liked them because they were torn and folded as though a great deal of attention had been paid to them. I sifted through the pile of papers and handed my mother her version of *Sweet Bird of Youth*. It was a ritual we had. My mother would assume the role of Princess Kosmonopolis and would read her lines with a thick accent. Sometimes, if he wasn't busy, my father would play Big Daddy from *Cat on a Hot Tin Roof*. He was much more dramatic than Mother—his performance comical and forced—to entertain me. My mother's performance was different. For her it was the real thing—even to an audience of one.

Back in Cleveland, my mother threw parties, and her friends would drink and start reciting Shakespeare, their booming stage voices becoming louder with every martini and cigarette. This was the first year my mother hadn't put me to bed before a party. In past years, I often sat on the stairs watching, but this year I hoped if I made myself useful, she would let me stay up, so I cleaned and polished and tried to look busy all day. She relented and let me dress up. All the cleaning had left me so tired that I was dead asleep on the chair in the study by 11:00 p.m.

Before nodding off, I remember a blond woman asking my mother about Tennessee Williams being in the audience when she played Blanche in *A Streetcar Named Desire* in Chicago. The blonde asked her what he had said to her about her performance. My mother was looking at me when she answered, "He didn't say anything." And then she covered me with a blanket.

After the party, I began to dream of Tennessee Williams. In my dreams, he sat in one of the thinly worn crushed-velvet seats in the front row of an ornate theater. He always wore a white, wrap robe with a gold logo on the breast pocket, like the kind you get in better hotels. I'd read the lines to him as my mother did, not committing too much of myself to the dialog, holding something back. "Always hold something back," my mother cautioned me. She said this kept the audience wanting more.

After I said my lines, Tennessee would speak to me from his seat. "You're positively marvelous, Margaret."

I'd curtsy like my mother taught me with my hands crossed and resting on my lap.

"Margaret," he would say.

"Yes?" I'd ask.

"You look just like your mother."

The next morning I told my mother I had decided to write a play. I'd ask my cousins to act in it.

My mother was preoccupied on the phone, but she put her hand over the receiver. "It's good to see you playing with your cousins. Someday you'll see that they aren't so bad." She handed me a pencil and motioned for me to go to the porch so she could finish her conversation. I figured it must be a friend from Cleveland because I heard her talking about the playhouse. "I can't," I heard her say. She was twirling the phone cord like a teenager. She sat on the chair and stretched her pale legs out, her toes touching the kitchen counter. "Of course I do." We never took calls at the summer house. Long-distance calls were expensive and reserved for special occasions only, plus half of the houses had party lines. I gathered my pencil and paper in my hands and flashed her an impatient look. "Noel ... no." I heard her shushing him. I walked out to the porch letting the screen door slam loudly behind me, but she never looked at me.

It took me a week or so to write my fifteen-page play. I scrawled the dialogue on several pieces of my father's old notebooks. After he saw I was serious, he gave me his manual typewriter—an old, black Underwood and some purple carbon paper to make copies.

"Here," he said, expertly swinging the carbon paper in the drum of the typewriter and slapping the metal bar into place. "Is the seat high enough?" He pulled at the old chair, and I went up and down until he found a spot that seemed perfect to him. He slid me into place in front of the typewriter.

"What do I do?" I looked up. The purple paper and the typewriter seemed to loom.

He sat on the desk next to me and looked down. "Is this too much?"

"I don't know." I looked up. "Maybe." I suddenly felt small in his office, sitting at his desk and in his chair with my fingers positioned on the cold keys and no idea of what to do next.

"Have you written it down on paper yet?"

I shook my head.

"Oh." He looked serious for a moment and put his fingers to his lips like he was concentrating. He went over to his briefcase and brought me a long, yellow pad of paper. He ripped off two sheets. "Start with these first, and when you fill them, you can read them to me, and we can type them onto the carbon paper."

I nodded obediently and took a pencil from the cup. When I looked up a minute later, he was gone.

By contrast to my mother who never did anything without a flair for the dramatic, my father moved through the house quietly. That was just the way he was. He was also a recovering alcoholic, and while my mother talked about plays and writers, I would hear my father often talk about the recovery process with his friends who were also recovering. Finally, I got up the courage one day to ask when he was going to be fully recovered. He looked at me with a bit of amazement.

"Never." He walked away from me and turned back for emphasis. "Never."

I couldn't imagine "never."

At dinner that evening, he brought up my play. "You should study some of the greats," he added. "Sartre, Ionesco, O'Neill ..."

My mother snorted at his suggestion.

He seemed wounded. "What on earth could possibly be wrong with that?"

"We have enough people in this house with their heads in books, don't you think?" She smiled and stabbed her broccoli floret.

"What does that mean?"

She looked down at her plate. "I'm just saying that you shouldn't stifle her by theorizing everything. She doesn't have to study anything or anyone. Just let her write her goddamn play, Gerald. That's all." She wiped her mouth with her napkin like she had eaten something distasteful.

There was no more talk of the great playwrights. Both of my parents focused intently on their chicken cutlets until my mother changed the subject and asked about the weather. After dinner, Father shut the door to his office. Soon, the typewriter began ticking.

My mother watched him shut the door, walked over to the record player, and put on an old Patsy Cline record. She turned up the volume until the ticking sound on the typewriter was drowned out. After gathering her long hair into a ponytail, she started singing along to "Walkin' after Midnight" while she filled the sink with dirty dishes. I went to help her, but she shook her head.

"Go ahead and write. I'll handle these." She smiled at me and began plunking cups into a steamy pool of soapy, blue water. I turned back to see her hips swaying underneath a blue sundress and thought she was the most beautiful woman I had ever seen.

I went out and sat on the porch. The air was crisp, and everything was quiet except for a June bug that kept smacking into the screen door.

At the end of the week, my father and I went to the library, and the head librarian made five copies of my play and returned them to me stapled. When she slid the stack over the counter to me, it looked real, like something Tennessee Williams would have written.

I sprang out of bed the next morning ready to perform my play. My father had promised to drive me down early to set up the stage area under the willow tree. I bounded out into the kitchen to find it empty. A quick inspection of all the rooms seemed to find everything neat and orderly and empty. I stepped onto the front porch to find Uncle Earl's truck pulling up in the driveway and my mother and father standing close just beyond the steps. For a moment, from the angle they were standing, I thought they were kissing, and then my mother turned her head and I saw that they were fighting. My father walked off down the path to the back of the house.

And that was when I spied it: the lone, large blue suitcase—the largest one of ours—sitting next to the driveway. It was the big one that held my mother's clothes and all of her shoes. My spirits jumped for a moment because I thought that maybe my wish had come true and that we were going back to Cleveland.

My mother hadn't noticed me and walked over to talk to Uncle Earl. She pointed to the suitcase. I wondered if the rest of the set was in the house and if somehow I had missed them. My mother looked beautiful in a crisp white shirt, checked scarf, black pants, and tortoise sunglasses. Her hair was gathered at the back of her neck in a ponytail, and her lipstick was one shade brighter than her hair. I remember this image of her vividly because it was the last one I would have of her for nearly a year.

She spied me and walked over to the porch. "I was just coming to find you." She motioned for one minute to Uncle Earl who nodded and climbed back into the truck. "Sit down for a minute." She pointed to the porch swing. "I got a great part in a play back home," she said. "It's too good to pass up. You understand, don't you?"

"I thought you had turned it down."

"I did at first." My mother sighed deeply.

"Which play?" I asked.

"It's a new one. Noel has written it himself. It's called *Revolution at Dawn*, and it's fabulous. Really, it is! No one has ever offered me a part like this."

"Not another Tennessee Williams play?" I asked.

"No. I'm getting a little tired of those, to be honest." She laughed. "This is something new. Noel is also directing it," she said. "You remember Noel, don't you?"

I ignored the concept of Noel. "Am I going with you?" I asked, eyeing her lone suitcase.

"No. I think it's best that you stay here with your father," she said. "I'm going to be rehearsing a lot, and the hours will be long, and there is talk that it could end up Off-Broadway. Isn't that exciting?"

She was performing for me. I had seen it before.

I wondered why my father wasn't here with her, assuring me that we would all be together again at the end of the summer. I wanted to hurt her for both my father and myself, so I chose my words carefully. "I guess you were right."

She looked puzzled. "About what?"

"It's time for me to grow up. I guess that starts today, huh?"

She looked disoriented for a moment and put her hands on her hips and stood up. She went to turn and then faced me and leaned down and gathered me in her arms. My face went into the soft spot of her neck where she sprayed her perfume.

"I love you," she said. She sniffled, but I didn't see if she was crying behind her sunglasses. "You remember that I love you."

I stood there stiff like I was made of wood. I was determined that I would hold something back of myself. Just like she had taught me. I heard Uncle Earl's truck start. She stood there with me, sniffling slightly until Uncle Earl yelled that she would miss her bus if she didn't hurry.

"You wrote a good play, Margaret," she said as she turned toward the truck.

I stood there and watched her leave. I should correct that; I walked to the middle of the road and watched her leave. I was hoping that she would turn and tell me to get out of the middle of the road and come back and realize that, without her, something terrible might happen to me. I wanted to hint at it, so I stood defiantly there on the yellow line on the dangerous curve around our rented house. The same road I was told to never—ever—go near. Maybe I was half hoping a truck would come and splat me all over the place, and she would see it all from the rearview mirror.

She and Uncle Earl had driven down the road about a mile when I felt a hand touch my shoulder. It was my father. "You're standing in the middle of the road, you know. Kind of dramatic, don't you think?"

I nodded. "Yeah, but I'm pretty pissed off."

"Me, too." He led me off the yellow lines and onto the yard. "I'm proud of you," he said. "Your play is good." He sat down on the top step of the porch. "I was thinking that you and I could go to Sewanee together. You could help me with my research if you wanted."

"I could study some of the great playwrights." My body heaved slightly as I fought the first tear. I rubbed my eyes hard. I hoped he'd think it was pollen. My mother always told me not to rub my eyes, but my father didn't know the things you say to a child. He had relied on my mother for such things.

We sat outside for twenty minutes in silence. He tried to speak to me, but gave up several times.

"She isn't coming back, is she?" I asked finally. I think I meant to Tennessee, but I think I knew that something larger was happening to my father and me that day.

"I don't know," he answered. "I don't think so."

I knew my father wouldn't recover from this, either. I finally understood that there were some things you just never get over.

"Come on," he said.

I smiled at him and watched him walk away. He was a tall man, and I liked the way his pants hung on his thin frame. He always wore wonderful clothes. I'm sure that's one of the reasons why my mother had loved him.

With Apologies to Rose Bonne [The Halls of Ives]

CEE

There were more damned beings at The Alamo, there
If you read works of fiction
Which, fiction should truly be said, "fictational"
Everyone with a story is a reporter, it seems
Every story about the battle
Until the battle
Is dictated, terbacky-chaw
Pull ye up a pickle barrel, pard, come learn about
The cat that was there
And the dog that was there
And the girl that was there
And the boy that was there
The 1836 populace of Poughkeepsie, it seems, all there
Wall to wall families with a mouse and a cat and a dog and a horse
The defenders died, of course

A Hindershot of Calion

Schuler Benson

April pollen draped the landscape like a chalky yellow gown, and the stuff was nickel-thick on the windshield of Dennis Shackleford's Oldsmobile. The car crept a slow roll over the last twenty or so feet of gravel leading up to the makeshift police barricade of two cars and a sawhorse in front of Crabapple Bait & Tackle. Sheriff Heidenreich sauntered around the hood of his tired Monterey, approaching the Oldsmobile and shaking his head. Denny thought the sheriff walked like a movie cowboy taught him how.

"Hello, Karl," Denny said, as he climbed out of his car and extended his hand. He ducked a wasp that buzzed by to rejoin one of the huge nests settled in the trees around Crabapple, hanging fat like upturned gourds of pine straw and parcel paper. The woods around Calion had a reputation for being choked with red wasps in spring and summer. They were out in full force.

"Denny," Heidenreich said. "Sorry to drag you out like this, but it's the damnedest thing I've had to deal with in a while, and, with it bein' the weekend, I wasn't sure who else I might give a holler."

"It's fine, friend," Denny said, still shaking hands. "How're May and Margot?"

"Good. They're good," Heidenreich said. "Jane?"

"Jane's fine; the girls are fine. Karl, what can I do for you?"

"Yeah, 'course, just a ..." Heidenreich patted down the pockets of his uniform, tapped the butt of his pistol, and then jutted both hands into his back pockets. "Winslow!"

"Uhyessir!" piped a red-faced, chubby deputy, as he trotted to Denny and Heidenreich from behind another patrol car.

"You got that note from earlier?" Heidenreich asked.

"Yessir." Winslow produced a sweaty, wrinkled piece of paper from his breast pocket. He handed it to Heidenreich, who handed it to Denny.

"Karl," Denny started, thumbing the corner of the folded note with his left hand, "I'm gonna do whatever I can for you here, but before I read this, I'd like to hear from you what, uh ... what we've got goin' on here."

"Arrite," Heidenreich said, lighting an unfiltered cigarette, prompting

Denny to do the same. "You know ole Hank Hindershot from out 'round Calion?"

"I may." Denny crossed his arms and clenched and unclenched his jaw, a process that'd helped him think since flying choppers in Korea. "Heard of the family, of course."

"Well—and I tell ya, Denny, this is just the damnedest thing—but Hank Hindershot is in that bait shop, and he's got some kind of damn bomb he's rigged up, and he says if the bank foreclosure on his timber stretch south of the river ain't reversed, he's gonna blow the damn thing up."

Denny pulled hard on his cigarette and looked the sheriff up and down. "Karl, are you feedin' me a line?"

Heidenreich chuckled. "That's the same thing I said when I got here. Winslow? What'd I say when I got here?"

"Sir?"

"What'd I say to ya when I got here?! Tell Mr. Shackleford!"

"Sir, he asked me if I was feedin' him a line," Winslow said to Denny.

"See?" Heidenreich said.

Denny replied, "Uh huh," then shook his head and spun the yellow note, still unopened in his hand. "Karl, why am *I* here?"

"Hell, I told you—I don't even know what direction to take this in! All 'emm Hindershot fellas got somethin' wrong with 'em, so I don't wanna take it too serious. But, on the other hand, if he's got a damn real bomb in there, we have us a problem!"

"If he blows up a bait shop?"

"Denny, he ain't alone in there. He says he got him some hostages."

"Who? How many?"

"Two. One's Kenny Foley, owns the place. The other's, uh ..." Heidenreich looked at his feet. "He says the other's Byrd Barton."

"Bullshit." Denny slid the note into his pocket and removed a small Swiss Army penknife.

"Yeah," Heidenreich said. "He says he's got the mayor."

Denny thought for a time, turning scenarios over in his head. Clench. Unclench. As he watched wasps dance along a nest hanging from one of the smaller pines across the road's drainage ditch, he clicked the file blade from his penknife and slid it along the underside of his fingernail whites. "Alright, Karl," he said, "who else've you called?"

"Just you."

"Okay. Well, who do you have that deals with explosives?"

"We have a, uh, a technician from the academy over in Camden. Not green like Winslow, but, still, he's just a trainee. He's waitin' for us to holler on the radio if we think we need 'im."

"You very well may. Go ahead and have him come on down."

Heidenreich nodded to Winslow, who ran in awkward strides to the radio in his cruiser.

Denny asked, "Have you called the FBI?"

"The FBI?"

"The FBI."

"Denny ... it's Sunday."

"It is."

"Well, Denny, you can't call the FBI on a Sunday."

"Mr. Shackleford," Winslow stage-whispered from his car, "I wouldn't wanna guess for certain as to whether or not the FBI's even open on Sundays."

"Denny," Heidenreich said, "we got a drunk in there who's prob'ly blowin' smoke, lookin' for attention, and hopped up on God knows what else. I called you down here because I figger you can just tell 'im to come on out, and he'll listen since you're a lawyer and people know you. Now, I trust you, and I known your brother thirty years. You tell me to take it serious, I will. But this ain't the kinda thing I'm best at, this tryin' to talk a man down. I know when to admit my faults, and this is one of 'em. You get 'em outta there."

"You say he's on something else? You know it?" Denny asked.

"Well, 'course, I can't say for certain, but I know all them fellas smoke marijuana 'round the lake."

"And we don't smoke it in Muskogee," Winslow added sternly.

"Forget it," Denny said, closing his knife and returning it to his pocket. "Alright, you're giving me the go-ahead to talk to this man, then? Realizing that if things go wrong, there's a possibility of a bad outcome?"

"Denny, just talk 'im down," Heidenreich said. "I don't wanna be sittin' across from you in a courtroom no more'n you want me tryin' to put you there."

"Okay, partner." As Denny walked back to his car, he ran a finger down the length of the Oldsmobile's sleek, midnight frame, crisscrossing chrome trim to form a single, pollenless snake of clean paint. Opening the back door and reaching inside, he called over his shoulder to the sheriff, "I see now why you asked me to bring this."

Denny pulled a three-foot-long, cream-white ceramic megaphone, with WILDCATS monogrammed down one side in purple cursive letters, and Carol down the other. The polished metal lip at its base gleamed in the sun like still water, and it smelled like lilacs. In the distance, he could see the lake glimmering through the sturdy pines surrounding the shop. Nubby rocks and dust ground beneath the soles of his cracked weekend loafers, as he paced back up to Heidenreich's cruiser. Apart from Denny's car and the sheriff's, the other vehicles were Deputy Winslow's patrol car, Kenny Foley's primer-gray Scout, and two pickups Denny didn't recognize. Heidenreich was fidgeting with his cruiser's rearview when Denny got back.

"Alright," Denny said, "let's pull one of the cars around to the side so we can talk to him through the window."

"Nossir," Winslow said. "Note said we can't come no closer."

"Then we'll be talking to a blank wall. Do you think he thought of that? Did you think of that?"

"I don't reckon."

"Alright, alright. So we talk to the wall. Now, which Hindershot is this? The streaker or the one who fights chickens?"

"Which one's the streaker?" Heidenreich asked.

"Might be the one who was gon' dam up the Ouachita on account of him havin' heard two rivers was better'n one," Winslow said.

"Good Lord," Denny sighed. He straightened his back and raised the megaphone to his mouth. "Hello in there! Hank Hindershot!"

There was no response. Heidenreich hooked his thumbs around his belt buckle. Winslow covered his left nostril with a finger, then blew out of the other until his face went mayhaw pink.

"Hank Hindershot!"

No answer. Denny shrugged. From the east side of the shop, the men heard the hitches and scrapes of a window screen being popped from its frame.

"Hello! Sumbitch!" came a shrill voice, country as cornbread.

"Am I speaking with Mr. Hindershot?" Denny spoke into Carol's echoic megaphone.

"Yeah, I'm him." The words were wet and garbled, like he was talking to Denny through a mouth full of rock salt. "Who're you?"

"Hank, my name's Dennis Shackleford. I'm a friend of Sheriff Heidenreich, and he's asked me to step in and talk to you about your demands."

"Shackleford?"

"Yessir."

"Like them lawyer Shacklefords from El Dorado?"

"That's right, I am. And I can be your lawyer after this, if you need me to."

Winslow whispered to the sheriff, "Ain't that a, uh, 'conflicted interest'?"

"Deputy," Heidenreich growled, "shut the hell up."

"Hell, I might could use me a lawyer," Hindershot shouted. "'Em boys out there tell you why I'm here?"

"They did. If I can lend a hand, I will, Hank."

"Yeah, we'll see 'bout that."

"I hear you got the mayor and Kenny Foley in there."

"Hunnert percent!"

Heidenreich and Winslow exchanged glances like two mutts hearing sirens.

Denny replied, "I'm gonna need to talk to 'em and be sure everything's okay."

"You gon' do what I say you're gon' do! All uh y'all son of a bitches!"

"We are," Denny said. "We certainly are. But the law's out here, Hank. They gotta know you're not sittin' in there with a couple dead fellas propped up in the meat locker."

For a moment, there was no response. Denny could hear muffled exchanges coming from inside the shop.

"Dennis Shackleford?" a new voice entered the colloquy.

"Yes, I'm Dennis Shackleford."

"Denny, Kenny Foley. I'm in here; Barton's in here. We're arrite."

"Mayor?" Denny shouted. "Can we hear from you?"

"Doubt it," Foley called. "Byrd been in here on my shine since two hours 'fore all this done started. He's on my floor in a heap."

"Bullshit," Heidenreich said to Denny. "That don't cut it."

"Sounds odd," Denny said into the megaphone, nodding at the sheriff. "You say he's passed out drunk?"

"I do say that, as that is the damn case," Foley said.

"Kenny, that sounds ... odd—"

"Mr. Shackleford," Foley interrupted, "have you met the mayor?"

Denny and Heidenreich thought for a moment, and both lit on the idea that Foley's claim wasn't that odd at all.

"Alright, Kenny, we'll buy it," Denny said.

"Now, lemme te—ruuuagh meyeaeeah!" Foley screeched.

"Y'all alright in there?"

Foley yelled, "Sumbitch kicked me!"

"Tell 'im!" Hindershot said.

"Tell us what?" Denny asked.

"He wants y'all to know what we got in here, that he's serious. It's a bomb, I think, y'all. I think it's a real bomb," Foley said.

"Ain't bullshittin'!" Hindershot shouted.

"Alright, okay. It's all gonna be okay," Denny said. "Now, Hank, I need you to understand something. This is a Sunday, and there's only so much we can do. We wanna help you. Hell, I wanna help you. I do. But there's just no way we can get loan officers and whoever the hell else to open up the bank and the vaults, then come down here with some paperwork in the middle of the day on a Sunday."

"That don't confront me none! You got a problem!"

"Hank, do you know anything about me?"

"Do what, now?"

"When I tell someone I'll do something, I do it. I have friends. I have colleagues. I've worked with people who tell you I'm telling the truth. I want to help you, but you've got to gimme some room to breathe here."

Hindershot didn't respond.

"Hank?"

Silence.

"I don't like that I can't see you, Hank. Can I come to the window?"

"Keep yer distance!"

"Alright, alright. We're just lookin' at a blank wall out here, Hank."

"And I'm to take blame for how the Good Lord put this sumbitch shop up?"

"Well," Denny said slowly, "no, I, uh ... I s'pose Mr. Foley's to blame."

"All uh y'all can go get fucked, cain'tcha!" Foley screamed. "I was gon' shut down early today!"

From a few hundred feet down the road, Denny and the officers heard that radio-static gargle of tires on loose gravel as the bomb man from Camden arrived.

"Who's all else out there?" Hindershot yelled.

"Another officer," Denny said. "Don't panic, Hank. We just have somebody we need to talk to, and he may wanna ask you some things."

"Who's askin' me? You don't ask me nothin'! I tell you!"

"Just sit tight, Hank. We're gonna handle this bidness."

From the plain, black Ford sedan that joined the growing fleet outside Crabapple Bait & Tackle, a young man with a crew cut and a thick neck approached Denny and Heidenreich. Winslow made another awkward run from his cruiser to rejoin the group.

"Sheriff Heidenreich," the crew cut said, "I'm Don Marx. Hear you got a bomb."

"We may," Heidenreich said. They shook sweaty hands.

"Who's this?" Marx asked, nodding at Denny.

Denny extended his hand. "Dennis Shackleford."

"Denny's a lawyer down in town," Heidenreich supplied. "He's helpin' us talk to the fella inside."

"Has the fella said anything about the explosive?" Marx said.

"No," Denny said, "besides us knowing he's got one."

"Can I talk to him?"

"You can try. He's been fairly receptive so far. A little spry, but ... you know."

"Are we, uh," Marx said with a fake cough, "are we communicating with the bombmaking hostage taker with a, uh, cheerleader megaphone?"

"Go Cats," Winslow said.

"Arrite," Heidenreich snorted. "You ever done anything like this before?"

"Done plenty in the class," Marx replied. "Did some unofficial work in 'Nam."

"I see," the sheriff said. He looked at Denny, troubled. "Do what you need to do."

"Sir," Marx said, gesturing to Denny, "may I?"

"Sure, sure," Denny said, handing Carol's megaphone to the officer.

Marx pulled a small notebook from his back pocket, and, holding the megaphone between his knees, flipped to a marked page in the middle. He cleared his throat and looked at Heidenreich, who gave Marx a nod. Denny couldn't figure out if it were for confidence or approval. Marx raised the megaphone.

"Hello, suspect!" Marx began to stammer like a student athlete reading words from an acceptance speech. "My name. Is. Officer. Marx. And I am here to help you reverse—resolve your issue."

"Son, what the hell is this?" Heidenreich said, batting the megaphone away from Marx's face.

"Sir, this is what's in the manual."

"The manual, you say?"

"Maybe you better let me keep on with him," Denny offered.

Heidenreich grabbed the megaphone from Marx and handed it to Denny.

"Look, we need to know what he's got in there. That's all," Marx said.

Denny raised the megaphone. "Hank?"

"What kinda shit show y'all got goin' on out there?" Hindershot called.

"Hank, this fella wants to know about your bomb. Can you get Kenny to tell him about it? Just so he knows what we called him here for?"

"Ain't bluffin', I tell ya!"

"I know, Hank, I know. We gotta let this fella know, too."

After a few awkward seconds, Foley called out again: "Whatchall wanna know?"

Marx jerked the megaphone away from Denny, catching Denny's finger in the metal handle bolted to the side.

"God dammit," Denny hissed through his teeth. "Son, you don't have to snatch it."

"Sorry, sir," Marx said to Denny, then into the megaphone, eyes fixed like a sniper scope on his little black notebook, "Sir! What. Does. The dee-vice look like?"

"Do what, now?" Foley called.

"The dee-vice! Can you dee-scribe it to me?"

"Well, it'd appear to be four paint cans filled with perforatin' charges, and they all held together with what looks like the fan belt off a damn Chevy."

"Um," Marx said. He looked to Denny and to the sheriff, then flipped frantically through the manual. "A, uh. A what charge?"

"I say, 'a perforatin' charge'!"

"Uhhhuh," Marx brayed. "Sir! Can you tell me the technical name for the explosive?"

"The what, now?"

Marx threw his right hand up and sent the manual sailing into the woods. "The textbook name of the explosive!"

"Y'all goldbrickin' around out there?"

Marx lowered the megaphone. "I'm not familiar with a device like that," he said to Heidenreich. "He says 'percolatin' charges'? Um. I can't say I know exactly, what uh. It's just that I—"

"Well, ain't that about boar-tit worthless," Heidenreich said. "Son, step back. Go get in that car and stay there in case I holler atcha again. Don't come back over here. Lord. Worthless."

Marx handed the megaphone back to Denny, whose left middle

finger was already swelling. Marx walked back to his car, shoulders slung low under shame, in a far less officious capacity than the one that first brought him from the car.

"On our own," Denny said.

Heidenreich chirped and produced a flask from his hip pocket. He took a hard pull, then handed it to Denny, who followed suit. The two lit up more cigarettes.

"Hank," Denny said, smoke pluming from the mouth of his daughter's megaphone.

Hindershot called back, "What now?"

"How's the mayor?"

"Still flat on his backside like a ole lush!"

"We're gonna have to take a second to think about this. We gotta get a plan together. Something real. Something that'll work. But I'm tellin' you, Hank, I have got to talk to you face to face. I don't know how else to make this happen to everybody's satisfaction."

Hindershot mumbled something inside the building, and Denny thought he heard Foley talk back. The two voices bickered for several minutes, as Denny and Heidenreich burned down smokes in rapid succession.

"Arrite, now," Hindershot finally called. "You come up to this winda, but you stand on that side of the wall, hear? Don't be stickin' your damn noggin in here, or I'll blow this whole spot to Kingdom Come, and you gon' take that same ride we do! Do not try to get in here! Sumbitch!"

"Alright, Hank," Denny said. "That's A-okay. I'm gonna set the megaphone down, and I'm gonna come up. Here I come, Hank."

As Denny approached the bait shop, he felt a keen unease. Somewhere in the building in front of him, some homecooked bomb sat waiting, and all that separated him from the blast was the warped, rickety wood of Foley's shop walls. The gravel beneath his loafers gave way to thick grass, and with each step, a puff of sooty pollen breathed up from his footprints. When he reached the corner of the shop, he noticed on the ground what Hindershot must've had to break through in order to get the window screen loose: a broken piece of plywood, whitewashed, with TAKE A CHILD FISHIN scrawled in black paint. He got a few steps closer and announced himself.

"Hank?"

"Yeah, I'm here." Something was different about Hindershot's voice. He was hoarse from all the yelling, but he seemed softer at the same time.

"Alright, Hank, this is what I'd like to do."

"You got my ear, counselor, but all this is wearin' me 'bout old-denim thin. You better say somethin' good."

"I hope to, Hank. Listen to me. Banks don't just change their minds on foreclosures. If you owe 'em for the land you're on, you're gonna have to pay that money, and there's just no way they're gonna reverse it otherwise. Now, this is what I'll do for you, Hank. You stop this; you let the sheriff and his man in there, and I will talk to the bank president. Not a loan man, but the president. I'll see if he'll reconsider, and I will cosign on a loan with you in order to get another chance on this. Now, I'm not gonna pay your mortgage for you. Not one cent. I will stake my credit on it, and my credit is excellent, but that's as far as I can go. I got a family, too. Hank. How's that sound?" Denny could hear Hindershot breathing around the corner.

"Don't need your lawyer money, and I don't want your credit," he said.

Denny edged as close to the building as he could, then peeked around the corner to look at the window from the side. Hindershot was close. Denny could see two sets of tan, rough fingers gripping the outer edge of the windowsill.

Denny leaned back to sound farther away. "Hank, this is a hell of a deal. More than you're gonna be able to get on your own, and more than even the sheriff was willing to give you before I came down here. Don't throw this back at me. Let me help you, and let's end this."

"It ain't about the damn money!"

Denny watched blood flee Hindershot's fingers as they tightened on the splintered, wooden sill. An opportunity arose, and Denny took it. He leaped from around the house and grabbed the two hands, shifting his weight backward and giving all he had to pulling Hindershot from the window. As Denny tumbled, his six-foot frame gained momentum, but it wasn't enough. Hindershot's wrists slipped free like wet soap, and his hands jerked back like Denny was a hot iron. Denny scrambled to get up and around the side of the shop, but when he reached his knees, his vision was framed by the barrel of a revolver.

"Easy," Denny stuttered. "Easy now."

Out of dusty shadows leaned a face Denny didn't expect: tanned, oily skin taut with tension and fear and anger, punctuated by wide eyes, blue as a Confirmation Bible.

"Get your sorry ass back to them cars," Hindershot said. "We're done with this. You get me somebody else. Somebody with juice. I have the mayor in here, man! You screwloose?! On your feet! Get the hell outta here!"

Denny stood, arms raised high, and walked slowly back toward the barricade where Heidenreich and Winslow waited, guns drawn.

"Well, Denny, what was that?" Heidenreich asked.

"I thought there was a chance. I took it."

"You almost got damn shot."

"I know. I know. But this changes things."

"Sure as hell, it does! Can't tell 'im nothin' now!"

"No, that's not what. ... Look here," Denny said. "That's not Hank Hindershot."

"Do what, now?" Heidenreich said.

"That is not Hank Hindershot in there," Denny said. "It's just some kid!"

"Like, a truant kid?" Winslow asked.

Heidenreich put his hands on his greasy forehead and began massaging his hairline.

"Karl," Denny said. "Karl! Listen, I couldn't be sure 'til now, but I have met Hank Hindershot before. Him and Hal, and I think Harmon, too. It was years ago, at a livestock auction. That in there—that ain't Hindershot. Looks like Hank a little. I think. ... Does he have kids?"

"Hell, I suppose he does, yeah. Yeah! Hard to keep 'em straight, but I know Hal's got at least three."

Winslow added, "Sheriff, we've picked up Hal's oldest at Hill's, hustlin' billiards a number of times."

"Jesus," Heidenreich said. "Well, what does this change?"

"He said it wasn't about money," Denny said.

"Whussat?"

"Money. The kid said that this wasn't about money."

"The bank thing?"

"Yeah. Listen, I think maybe we can wrap this up a different way now, but this is still a delicate situation."

Denny glanced back to see Marx sitting on the hood of the sedan. Marx noticed Denny looking and shrugged, raising his hands. Denny waved him off and looked at Heidenreich and Winslow.

"One more thing to remember," Denny said, "is he's got a pistol in there, Karl."

"Did you see Barton?"

"No, I didn't see anything but a barrel in my face and a kid pointing it."

"I s'pose if he'd shot nobody, we'd've heard it," Winslow said.

"I suppose," Denny said, glaring at the deputy, "but somethin's not adding up here. If money's not the problem—and that's just one of the Hindershot kids in there—I just don't see why we're all here. What's he care about his daddy's land? Or his uncle's, or whoever's it is?"

"Mr. Shackleford," Winslow said, "you say he ain't that old. How old?"

"Couldn't be more than eighteen," Denny said. "I'd be surprised if he was outta high school. Hell, he looks like my oldest's boyfriend."

"Huh," said Winslow.

Heidenreich asked, "What's on your mind, Deputy?"

"Well, just him bein' a kid. Reminds me of bein' a kid out here, and uh, I think maybe I got a idea 'bout how we can flush 'em all outta there."

"Well, Mr. Winslow, we're all ears," Denny said.

"Uh huh," Winslow replied. "Y'all think 'at bomb fella's got any kinda, say ... bomb-protection clothes or some such various 'n' sundry items?"

Denny and Heidenreich sat inside the sheriff's patrol car and watched through the windshield as Winslow emerged from behind Marx's sedan. The deputy was decked head to foot in Camden Academy's police-issued bomb-protection gear, which Denny recognized as a ball-catcher's mask and pads. Winslow carried a gaff pole he'd pulled from the back of Foley's truck, and on the end of it hung the biggest wasp nest Denny had ever seen. Even with Winslow as far off and moving as slow as he was, through the patrol car's cracked windows, Denny and Heidenreich could hear the buzzing growing louder. Winslow neared the edge of the building where Denny first spoke to the kid. The deputy, still looking toward the shop, put his left fist next to his head, and raised two fingers, signaling to Denny and Heidenreich to take their positions. The two quietly exited the car, leaving their doors open, and crept up the footworn path to the opposite side of the bait shop, approaching the front entrance. They knelt by the driver's side back wheel of Foley's truck and waited. On the opposite corner, Winslow slowly reared back his gaff pole, and in one quick, smooth arc, flung the nest through the window and into the bait shop.

"Red Baron! Red Baron!" Winslow yelled, his voice wavering up and down like an air-raid siren.

The reaction was instant.

From inside the shop, Foley screamed first: "Myeeaaaap! Sumbitch, sweet Holy Jesus!"

Foley came barreling through the front door, his round gut bouncing beneath his shirt like he was carrying a piglet in an apron. Behind him, waving a pistol, ran a skinny kid, a few inches shorter than Denny, and behind the kid, a frantic swarm of red leaders. As Foley and Hindershot looped around the hood of the truck, Heidenreich popped to his feet and grabbed the kid by the back of the shirt collar, jerking the boy down to the dirt. Denny heard the whoosh of air leaving lungs, and the kid lay on his back squirming and breathless. Heidenreich pulled his own revolver.

Winslow came trotting around the far side of the bait shop, still dressed as a minor leaguer, with his drawn sidearm in one hand and a plume-spewing smoke grenade in his other. He tossed the fogger into the bait shop and stood clear of the door, counting aloud, "One Mississippi, two Mississippi ..."

"Lemme up, dammit!" the kid screamed at Heidenreich. "I got a allergy!"

"And I got a pistol!" the sheriff said. He put one foot on the kid's chest and leaned.

"Pull me back; I got a allergy! I got a allergy!"

"Karl!" Denny said. "Grab his ankles!"

Denny grabbed the kid's wrists, kicking Hindershot's unhanded revolver back toward the front of the shop. Heidenreich took up the boy's lower end, and they followed Winslow—who'd stopped counting at "Twenty Mississippi"—back into Crabapple Bait & Tackle.

"Y'all crazy son of a bitches!" Foley yelled from back near Marx's sedan. "A flurry uh sumbitch wasts in my shop! Y'all son of a bitches, ever'one!"

"He just a-sawin' logs," Winslow said, as he knelt by Mayor Barton, who remained comfortably passed out on a pile of lifejackets near the shop's front counter. On the counter, by a tan cashbox and a display of slick, black lures, sat a square piece of plywood to which were bolted four full-sized paint cans, lashed together with a rubber fan belt. From the tops of each can trailed thick fuses that met in the middle in a single fat braid. Denny and the sheriff stood over the kid, who lay whimpering and cursing as he leaned against a shelf of cricket buckets.

"I am Hank Hindershot," he spat. "I'm the third."

"Well that figgers," Heidenreich said.

"Son," Denny said, "what the hell have you done here?"

"Look, damn y'all, it ain't my fault my deddy and his deddy and all 'em sumbitches is drunks and worthless! That stretch is my stretch, and that timber is mine. I got money to pay what's owed to the bank man! Done worked since I was thirteen, knowed it was comin' someday. Didn't think it'd be now, but it come! I go see them fellas at the bank two weeks ago, and they bound and determined to not take my money. Hell, I tried to pay 'em! All I wanna do is keep what's mine! We already got three acres laid rot out there on account a'cuz my deddy got in the bottle and let it all go! I just wanna harvest my timber and keep what's mine!"

"A Hindershot that don't get a fair shake," Heidenreich joked. "Lo and behold. Somebody hold me up."

"Piss on you!" Hindershot yelled, shooting spittle.

"Alright!" Denny shouted, patting Heidenreich on the shoulder, pacifying him. Denny turned and walked to the counter. He pulled his knife from the pocket of his trousers and used the wedge to pop the top from one of Hindershot's paint cans. He looked inside, shook his head, and replaced the lid.

"It's just paint," he announced, as Hindershot frowned, furrowing his brow and curling his hands into trembling fists, and Heidenreich scoffed. "Son," Denny said to the pouting kid, "do you really have the money the bank needs?"

"Every red cent."

"Mm. Karl." Denny looked to the sheriff. "What charges does Hindershot the Younger, here, face?"

"Sweet Jesus, Denny, we're 'bout where I toldja we were when ya got here." Heidenreich swung open the cylinder of Hindershot's recovered revolver. "Ain't no bullets in this pistol. If it ain't nothin' but paint in them cans, and ain't nobody here hurt, and Foley ain't gon' press charges for the damages to his place—"

"I should press some damn charges on all uh y'all son of a bitches!" Foley heaved breathlessly from the front door.

"Well, hell, Kenny, why don't you just do that?" Heidenreich said. "Tell ya what, I'll help ya. We can g'on 'head file a insurance claim for the damage while we're at it. And after they come fix the shop up, why not send 'em back to that shed about thirty foot past the tree line out there? See if they can't work on it some, too."

"Do what, now?"

"Well, Kenny, that shed that I know about that you think I don't know about."

"Now, wait just a damn minute, Sheriff," Foley whimpered. "As I look around, it occurs to me ain't too much broke anyway that didn't need fixin' as is." He moped like a sullen runt as he grabbed a small, red toolbox from a shelf and headed for the front door. "Godamighty."

"As I say, if Foley don't press charges," the sheriff continued, "there ain't too much gon' happen."

"What about the mayor?" Winslow said.

"Hell, we can prob'ly stick 'im in his bed at home, and he won't never even know he was here."

"Alright, Hank," Denny said. "This is what we're gonna do. You're not your old man. I can respect that. Like I told you earlier, I've had my share of dealing with the bank in town. Tomorrow morning, I'm gonna go down there, and I'm gonna talk to the people I know about your situation. We're gonna have them take that money and give you back your land. You're gonna go with Sheriff Heidenreich after this, and you're gonna spend the night in lock-up, and there's not a single thing anybody's gonna do about that. But you'll be arraigned in court tomorrow or Tuesday, and when that happens, I'll be there to represent you."

"I can't pay nothin'," Hindershot said. "All I got's gotta go to the bank."

"Oh, you're gonna pay," Denny said. "You're gonna pay with that paint right there, because I got a whole back side of my house we just added on to, and I've been waitin' for a deal just like this one. If it takes you a year of workin' weekends around workin' your timber, you will paint every stick and then some."

Heidenreich lifted Hindershot from the ground, pulling the boy's wrists behind his back and cuffing them.

"Mr. Shackleford," the kid said, "I ain't my deddy."

"I'm countin' on that, son."

The sheriff walked him out and into the back of the patrol car. Denny walked over to the counter and wrapped the paint cans, still attached to plywood, in a burlap cloth that lay beneath the board. As he lifted the parcel, Mayor Byrd Barton stirred.

"I would appear to find myself upon a damn floor," Barton slurred groggily.

"Evenin', Mayor," Denny said.

"Dennis Shackleford?"

"Yessir, Mr. Mayor."

"Why, hello, Dennis. Anything bitin' on the water today?"

"More'n you can shake a stick at." Denny walked out of Foley's shop, back to the trunk of his Oldsmobile.

"Karl," Denny said, shaking hands with the sheriff.

"Denny. Hell of a day, my friend."

Winslow exchanged baseball equipment and pleasantries with the Camden cadet as Foley huffed at the side of his shop, hammering his TAKE A CHILD FISHIN sign over the broken window.

"One to tell the kids about," Denny said.

"Hell, Denny, I ain't gonna tell nobody about this."

"Me, either," Denny laughed.

"Tell Jane and the girls we say hello, and gimme a holler if there's anything you need. I'm sure I'll be seein' you in court for this one." Heidenreich pointed his thumb at Hindershot, who sulked in the back of the sheriff's car. "Careful, Denny. Another ne'er-do-well Hindershot from Calion."

"Anyone ever bail you out, Karl? Give you another shot," Denny said, slowly adding, "Sheriff?"

Heidenreich grinned and looked at the ground, nodding. "Better say hello to Marshall for me, too."

"My best to May and Margot," Denny added, as Heidenreich started up his patrol car. Through the window, Denny could make out Hindershot mouthing, *Thank you.*

"It is a beautiful evening," Mayor Barton said, when he finally staggered from the front of Crabapple Bait & Tackle. "Foley! I seem to've left my billfold at the house, so I'm gonna hafta getcha for the bottle and the crickets on Tuesday."

"Son of a bitches," Foley muttered. "Son of a bitches, all uh y'all. Ever'one."

Jane picked up after the third ring.

"Hey, honey," Denny said.

"Hey, Den. Gonna be a late one?"

"No, ma'am. I'm just about wrapped up at the office. Headed home shortly. Just wanted to give a holler."

"Okay. The girls are home. Everything turn out alright today?"

"I s'pose. Thinkin' of the girls. I'm grateful."

"Oh, are you?" Jane chuckled.

"Yes, ma'am." He smiled. "I don't think I've got a tolerance for young men. They're just ... crazy."

"Come on home, Den."

"Yes, ma'am. Be that way soon. One quick stop to make first."

Denny placed the receiver back in its cradle and walked out of the offices he shared with Marshall on the third floor of the building downtown. He took the front exit out to his Oldsmobile and headed a few blocks away to the new building on Church Street. Aside from some of the interior trim, plumbing, and a bit of electrical work, the new firm was nearly done. He pulled into the red-brick-partitioned private parking area they'd set aside to the east of the building, got out of his car, and unlocked the side door that would eventually lead straight to the private offices. He followed the hallway to the partners' lounge and winked at Marshall's seven-foot marlin they'd mounted as a centerpiece. No furniture yet, but the marlin was in place. Denny passed through the nearly completed bathroom to a small doorway leading down a set of stairs into the basement they'd built, about which neither Marshall, Norwood, nor Denny told anyone. Leaving all the doors open, he returned to his car, opened the trunk, and removed his heavy, burlapped parcel. Making his way through the darkness, Denny tiptoed carefully through halls and doorways, down the stairs, into the small basement, to the far back corner, directly beneath the office that would be his. He placed the parcel in the corner and turned to go, feeling his way along walls, up stairs, past the marlin, and back out to the car, lighting a cigarette as he climbed in.

Driving home, Denny slid his hand into his pocket, removing Hindershot's wrinkled note. He took two hard pulls on his smoke, then put the note to the tip. Denny thought of youth while the paper caught fire. He thought of the future. He thought of his wife, his three daughters, and Hank Hindershot III. He thought of the four paint cans packed to the rims with dynamite in the basement of his new law firm. Denny extended his hand from the car window and let wind take the note. He saw it flicker in the rearview as it hung like a feather in his wake, still burning. Denny thought and drove. Clench, unclench. On into the night.

Author Biographies

SCHULER BENSON
had first book, *The Poor Man's Guide to an Affordable, Painless Suicide*, published by Alternating Current Press in 2014. He is a doctoral candidate in the Composition and Rhetoric program at the University of South Carolina, where he also teaches writing.

MIKE BERNICCHI
is an American poet, teacher, and soldier currently deployed in an undisclosed location. He enjoys throwing rocks at random objects to pass the time, fighting wars for corporate profit, and watching the same movies on his iPad repeatedly when he is not on mission.

GAVIN BROOM
is originally from Central Scotland and now lives and writes in Michigan. He's been published over sixty times both online and in print and, in a very focused world tour, has read at Dire Literary Series in Boston, at Last Monday at Rio in Glasgow, Scotland, and at the Michigan State University Creative Writing Open Mic. His debut novel, *The Scottish Book of the Dead*, was published by Island City Publishing in 2018, and is available online or from the trunk of his car.

MARY BUCHINGER
is author of *e i n f ü h l u n g / in feeling* (2018), *Aerialist* (2015), and *Roomful of Sparrows* (2008). She is President of the New England Poetry Club and Professor of English and Communication Studies at MCPHS University in Boston; her work has appeared in *AGNI*, *DIAGRAM*, *Gargoyle*, *Nimrod*, *Salamander*, *Slice*, and elsewhere. Find her at marybuchinger.com.

JARED A. CARNIE
currently lives in Sheffield, England. He was awarded a Northern Writers Award in 2015 and his debut novel, *Waves*, was published in 2016. He can be found at jaredacarnie.com.

KEVIN CATALANO
is the author of the novel, *Where the Sun Shines Out* (Skyhorse). His writing has appeared in *Pank*, *Fanzine*, *Gargoyle Magazine*, *storySouth*, and other places. He teaches at Rutgers University-Newark, and lives in New Jersey with his wife and two kids. Stalk him at kevincatalano.com.

CEE
is the author of 27 chapbooks, holds a Pushcart nomination, saw publishing of over 1,000 poems and a regular column, all in the past decade. He fails to see what else he's expected to do. It's not like he ever got that flying DeLorean.

MICHAEL COOPER
is an Inland Empire poet, PoetrIE member, MFA student, veteran, and father of two great sons: Markus and Jonathan. His work is in *Tin Cannon, The Pacific Review, The Chaffey Review, The Camel Saloon, The Los Angeles Review, H_NGM_N, The Berkeley Review, The Portland Review*, and other fine (but wild) publications.

MIA EAKER
lives and writes in Charlotte, North Carolina. She received her MA in English from the University of North Carolina at Charlotte, where she currently teaches composition. Mia is a Lecturer in UNCC's University Writing Program.

J. LEWIS FLEMING
is a writer, poet, playwright, once and future editor, and father. All of these cause him more than a little frustration, and enough joy that he occasionally is overwhelmed by it all. He has been fortunate enough to have two titles of poetry, *The Bones of Saints Under Glass* and *Shades of Green*, published by Alternating Current.

ANDREI GURUIANU
writes work that often explores such topics as memory and forgetting and the ability of place to shape personal and collective histories. He currently teaches in the Expository Writing Program at New York University.

STEVE KARAS
is the author of *Kinda Sorta American Dream* (Tailwinds Press, 2015) and *Mesogeios* (WhiskeyPaper Press, 2016). His stories have appeared in *Necessary Fiction, Hobart, JMWW, Little Fiction*, and elsewhere. He lives in Chicago with his wife and two kids, and recently completed his first novel.

NOEL KING
lives in Tralee, Co. Kerry, Ireland, and has published more than a thousand poems, haiku, or short stories in magazines and journals in 38 countries. His poetry collections are: *Prophesying the Past* (2010), *The Stern Wave* (2013), and *Sons* (2015). Find him at noelking.ie.

STEPHANIE LIDEN
was born and raised in Northern Minnesota. She received her B.A. in journalism and her M.A. in English from the University of North Dakota, where she completed her thesis-style portfolio, a critique of popular immigration narratives in American Literature. She contributed as a reader for *North Dakota Quarterly* and the student-run literary magazine, *Floodwall*.

ALEXA MERGEN
studied writing and literature at UC-Berkeley, UC-Irvine, and George Washington University. Originally from Washington, D.C., Alexa has lived in Germany, Michigan, West Virginia, and California, and has crossed the United States by train and car several times. She makes her home in Ely, Nevada.

Normal
remains "one of the last American primitives" in the underground press, with presently 600 pieces published between 1992 and 2019 (without the Internet). His most recent book, *I See Hunger's Children: Selected Poems 1962–2012*, was published by Lummox Press.

Charles P. Ries
lives in Milwaukee, Wisconsin. His work has appeared in over 200 publications and is archived at Marquette University. He has received five Pushcart Prize nominations and is the author of *The Fathers We Find*, a memoir, and six books of poetry, including *Girl Friend & Other Mysteries of Love*. Find him at minktronics.com.

Constance Sayers
received an M.A. in English from George Mason University. Her fiction appeared in *Souvenir* and *Amazing Graces* and was nominated for a Pushcart Prize and Best of the Net. She is an executive at Atlantic Media (publisher of *The Atlantic*) and co-founder of the *Thoughtful Dog* literary magazine.

Eric Shonkwiler
is the author of *Above All Men*, *8th Street Power & Light*, and *Moon Up, Past Full*. He is the winner of a Coil Book Award and a Midwest Connections Pick by the Midwest Independent Booksellers Association. He was a Chancellor's Distinguished Fellow at the University of California-Riverside and a New River Gorge Winter Writer-in-Residence in West Virginia.

John Vicary
has been a contributor to more than 60 compendiums in his career and is a Pushcart-nominated author. He is the submissions editor at Bedlam Publishing and also cofounded the editing business The LetterWorks. He enjoys playing piano and lives in rural Michigan with his family. You can read more of John's work at keppiehed.com.

Sarah Ann Winn
had her first book, *Alma Almanac* (Barrow Street, 2017), win the Barrow Street Book Prize, selected by Elaine Equi. She teaches poetry workshops in Virginia, and online at the Loft Literary Center. She is Reviews Editor for *Tinderbox Poetry Journal*. Visit her at bluebirdwords.com or follow her at @blueaisling.

Amy Wright
is the author of two poetry books, one collaboration, and five chapbooks. Her writing has also won the Writers at Work contest, two Peter Taylor Fellowships to the *Kenyon Review* Writers Workshop, an Individual Artist Grant from the Tennessee Arts Commission, and a VCCA fellowship.

Pete M. Wyer
is a composer and musician from England with an interest in storytelling and innovation. He has created scores for the London Symphony Orchestra, Royal Philharmonic Orchestra, Juilliard, the orchestra of Welsh National Opera, The Crossing, BBC Television, and the Royal Opera House, as well as creating seven operas and music theater works.

Acknowledgments

Alternating Current wishes to acknowledge the following publications where pieces from this collection first appeared: "Kinda Sorta American Dream" was previously published in *Little Fiction* and in the story collection, *Kinda Sorta American Dream* (Tailwinds Press). "Inheritance" was previously published in *Control Literary Magazine*. "Coralee Robbins Mafficks the Fall of Art" was previously published under a different title in the poetry book, *Cracker Sonnets* (Brick Road Poetry Press). "Sculpting Sand" was previously published in the story collection, *Kinda Sorta American Dream* (Tailwinds Press). "Tennessee" was previously published in *Souvenir*.

Colophon

The edition you are holding is the First Print Edition of this publication.

All titles and drop capitals are set in Intimacy, created by Emerald City Fontwerks. All secondary lettering, subtitles, and interior text are set in Athelas, created by José Scaglione and Veronika Burian. The swash cursive font of the cover and title pages is set in Champignon, created by Claude P. The section separator graphic is set in Bergamot Ornaments, created by Emily Lime Design. The Alternating Current Press logo is set in Portmanteau, created by JLH Fonts. All fonts are used with permission; all rights reserved.

The Alternating Current lightbulb logo was created by Leah Angstman, ©2013, 2019 Alternating Current. The Luminaire Award medallions were created by SuA Kang and Devin Byrnes of Hardly Square, hardlysquare.com, for Alternating Current's sole use. All graphics are used with permission; all rights reserved.

Front cover artwork: "Falling in Love." Artwork by Loui Jover. Property of and ©2019 Loui Jover. Used with permission; all rights reserved. Find him on Instagram at @louijover, at saatchiart.com/louijover, and at facebook.com/lojoverart.

The editors wish to thank the font and graphic creators for allowing legal use.

Other Works from
ALTERNATING CURRENT PRESS

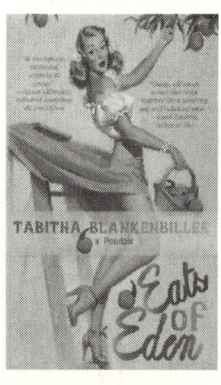

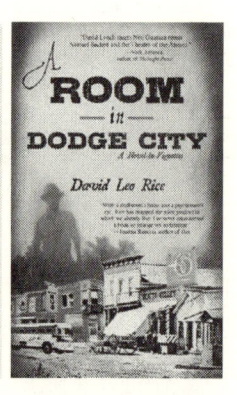

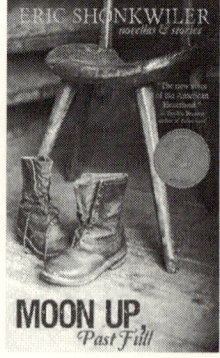

All of these books (and more) are available at Alternating Current's website: press.alternatingcurrentarts.com.

ALTERNATINGCURRENTARTS.COM